ALSO BY PHIL ROSS

BOTCHED BLOODING
They Tried to Kill Me ... And Then They Stole My Livelihood
A Fictionalized Account of Compelling Actual Events

ONCE A TROJAN
ALWAYS A TROJAN
A True Story

BLUE HOMBRES

THE LIFE AND TIMES OF MAJOR LEAGUE BASEBALL'S LATINO UMPIRES

First of a Trilogy

PHIL ROSS

TO CARM!
THANX FOR THE
INTEREST,
ENJOY!
Phil
Ross

TRail's End Press©
DENVER

ISBN-13: 978-1533058805
ISBN-10:1533058806

TABLE OF CONTENTS

INTRODUCTION

Orgullo.

   Pasión.

   Fidelidad.

   Devoción.

   Precisión.

Simple, single words: Pride, passion, loyalty, commitment, accuracy.

Like the many condiments and exotic spices required to create the ultimate *salsa*, they blend together to weave a coat of honor – a blue vestment signifying one of sport's most noble, yet misunderstood, professions. The baseball umpire – at every level from T-ball, through Little League, high school, college, the minor leagues and right up to the pinnacle of the major leagues – is, other than the players, managers and coaches, the definitive necessary ingredient in an enduring, worldwide pastime. Ever-threatened to be completely replaced or partly supplanted by one state-of-the-art robotic device or another, the flesh-and-blood umpire keeps a nonetheless-near-perfect human element involved in officiating.

Despite the obvious necessity of the Man in Blue, however, he (increasingly, also *she*) is no doubt the most reviled character in baseball, regardless of level of play. While statistics repeatedly, year after agonizing year, have proved umpires to be accurate most of the time, the comparatively few calls they miss are those grabbing the most attention, and therefore causing the most controversy.

The advent of instant review in the 2015 season in Major League Baseball (MLB) was controversial, and probably caused some MLB arbiters to down a few extra swallows of *Maalox®* or *Pepto Bismol®*. Yet, despite any anxiety, the same statistical probabilities – even in this age of ultra-comprehensive Sabermetrics and those review cameras – have amplified the center-of-the-bullseye accuracy of umpires who have earned the distinction as regular call-makers in The Show, a term familiar to anyone who has watched the movie, *Bull Durham*.

During the post-World War II era are anywhere between a dozen and 15 – the exact number is arguable – MLB umpires of Latino descent who became part of those barking out ball, strike, safe, out, fair, foul, interference, obstruction or balk decisions on every pitch or swing of the bat.

There exist literally hundreds of instances during the average nine-inning game where these proud *Blue Hombres* patrolling the base paths must render spur-of-the-moment verdicts.

One *non*-Latino major league umpire captured the deeper essence back in 2011, when he was part of an in-depth exercise conducted by a team of researchers from the Arizona-based Society for American Baseball Research (SABR). That is the group having created Sabermetrics – a statistical analysis of baseball data, in-depth and computerized, popularized in Michael Lewis's best-selling book, *Moneyball*, and the subsequent movie of the same name – which has filtered down into including every conceivable category to evaluate umpires.

"People only know to hate us. We are a misunderstood group. People don't really know us, but to know us is to love us," MLB umpire Phil Cuzzi told the SABR researchers.

Another longtime umpire who is non-Latino, yet who has mentored numerous *Blue Hombres* in his 33 years as a big league arbiter, unwittingly underscored Cuzzi's sentiments, reflecting on professional officials' inherent impartiality.

Following a New York Mets-Colorado Rockies series he and his three partners had just completed in May 2016, Crew Chief Gerry Davis was in the lobby of his Denver hotel on a Sunday afternoon, checking out to head to the airport for the crew's next assignment. When the author of this book, who had moments before finished a months-long series of interviews with him, casually inquired, "Where are you headed next, Gerry?" Davis quickly responded, "Baltimore." To which the author followed up, curiously, "Who are the Orioles playing?" To which the man who has called more than 4,000

MLB games, and more postseason contests than anyone, retorted, just as quickly, "Don't know, and don't care," as Venezuelan umpire/crew mate Carlos Torres stood next to his elder with a knowing grin.

Torres and the rest of the Latino contingent policing the sport in MLB ballparks across the United States, plus the one in Canada, are linked by an ancestral tongue, Spanish. Otherwise, the grouping has a diverse national origin that includes not only those "Born in the USA" but Latino umpires who hail from such *beisbol loco* locales as Mexico, Cuba, the Dominican Republic and, of course, Venezuela.

Accentuating the cultural and culinary differences among Spanish-speaking countries that have provided the big leagues with competent game-callers since the 1970s, one of the men, of Latino descent, yet U.S.-born, commented, "In my travels, when I shop to buy groceries for the three-day hotel stays that are common, I notice a lot of supermarket chains have an aisle for 'Hispanic' foods. Then I think how absurd that is," he said, flashing a knowing grin that masked inner disgust with the stereotyping of a diverse Latino populace bound primarily by a common native language of their forebears but not necessarily everything else.

"I mean, Mexican food has *tacos, enchiladas, tamales, chiles rellenos* and the like," the umpire began to explain, fashioning himself as somewhat of an international gourmet, based not solely on his shopping adventures in U.S. grocery stores but also time spent umpiring winter league games in the Dominican Republic, Venezuela and other baseball-bonkers Caribbean venues. He finished with a further afterthought: "Whereas the Cuban cuisine has, maybe, *ropa vieja* and *plátanos fritos*, and the Venezuelans have, say, *tequeños* or *pabellón criollo*."

***

The original pacesetter for Latino MLB umpires was the late Armando H. Rodriguez, a Havana, Cuba, native who died in 2008 at age 79 and was an American League umpire for two seasons in 1974-75. However, the really enduring Latino pioneer was Richard Raul "Rich" Garcia, born in the "Conch Republic" of Key West, Fla., just 90 miles across the water of the Straits of

Florida from Havana. Garcia was an AL umpire from 1975 until retiring in 1999. The lifelong Floridian added the title of Crew Chief to his balls-and-strikes résumé in 1985.

Beginning with the 2000 season, the American and National leagues consolidated umpires, who had been either AL or NL employees, into a single entity, the MLB Umpires Association, with John Hirschbeck elected as its first president, according to the official website, MLB.com. On Feb. 24 of that year, the World Umpires Association (WUA) was certified as the exclusive collective bargaining agent for all regular full-time major league umpires. Joe West, longest-tenured big league umpire as of 2016, with 34 years of service, and current union president, was elected to the WUA post in 2009.

The two major moves followed the threatened strike of unionized umpires, as dozens of members, unable to legally force a work stoppage, resigned, many getting reinstated two years later. The mass resignations, causing MLB to recruit replacement umpires for the '99 season, also ultimately resulted in several "replacements" being hired permanently.

That key transition also occurred long after the permanent demise of the fabled "balloon" chest protector, used exclusively in The Bigs by AL plate umpires up to the late 1960s or, at the latest, the early '70s, according to an unofficial consensus of serious baseball historians and other knowledgeable observers of the sport. By contrast, NL arbiters assigned to "the dish" had worn an inside chest protector, carefully positioned and secured underneath their uniform shirt, for much longer. The latter piece of protective gear has been the sole type of chest guard, then, for largely the past half-century – affording compactness, comfortability and better freedom of movement.

Another important side effect of the outside protector's eternal disappearance was the rudimentary difference in strike zones of old with the modern application. Even though rulebooks define the strike zone from a top spot at a horizontal line midway between the shoulder and belly button, and the bottom limit at another imaginary line in the hollow below the kneecaps … when a batter is in his normal stance, ready to receive a pitch, the human factor supersedes universal rulebook adherence.

Back in the day, long-ago AL veterans had "high" strike zones; they tended to call strikes on pitches as high as the rulebook definition of the upper boundary; this was basically because they became accustomed to peering down at the corners of home plate with their chins situated in the curvature at the top of the heart-shaped balloon protector when *they* were crouched in a stance, immediately outside a catcher's one shoulder, awaiting the next pitch.

Contemporary umpires over the past four decades or so, by contrast, are taught to have lower strike zones than their predecessors of what is essentially a bygone era – exclusively employing the inside chest protector, to which hard vinyl, contoured shoulder guards are attached to each side, designed to fit snugly inside shirt sleeves. Consequently, modern arbiters are prone to call pitches grazing the bottom of the knees as strikes, rewarding a pitcher who demonstrates consistency in "hitting spots" throughout a game.

Horizontally, this theory extends beyond the rubberized, Monopoly® house-shaped white triangle of home plate to the black-edged border; while that edge technically is not part of the 17-inch-wide plate, if a pitcher with good control consistently "paints the black" – a Rembrandt to baseball purists – a capable umpire will call a strike every time. In the professional give-and-take between players and officials, seasoned pitchers come to *know* precisely where to place a particular pitch with specific plate umpires – creating the grudging type of mutual respect that natural enemies like a cat and mouse develop towards one another in a fragile co-existence.

Depending strictly on personal preference, the three common stances for today's plate umpires, to enable the correct reaction and instant decision in the mere seconds it takes for a pitch to arrive, are:

- **The Box:** By far the most popular, with feet evenly planted flush with each shoulder, typically with the umpire's hands tucked between his legs for added protection, or more recently, the hands and forearms resting atop each thigh – the latter positioning offering a little less arm protection but more balance;

- **The Scissors:** One leg bent in a crouch, the other stretched out and protruding backward, hands resting one on top of the other on the lead leg, protecting the bottom hand better, yet leaving the top one, plus the elbows, more exposed;

- **The Knee:** Similar to the Scissors, but with one knee anchored against the ground, as a pitch is delivered. This has evolved to be the least-common.

While Major League Baseball allows its umpires individual personal discretion in choosing a stance when calling balls and strikes, most utilize the Box because it naturally positions a body with both the feet and shoulders creating a square.

Minor League Baseball (MiLB), conversely, wields a tighter rope with its generally much younger, still somewhat impressionable arbiters, who are eager to reach the peak of their profession, and anxious to please both their overseers and peers alike.

"We don't give our umpires an option. We teach only The Box in umpire school, so that's all our umpires use," said Miami, Fla., resident Jorge Bauzá. A "man who wears many hats," as he described his multiple roles, Bauzá, Puerto Rican by birth, boasts a two-part primary title of Field Evaluator/Instructor, MiLB Umpire Development, and Lead Rules Instructor, MiLB Umpire Training Academy, along with three other significant roles. "We want their shoulders square; the Box gives them the best method to achieve that goal.

"When they get called up (to the majors)," he added, the prospects are well-schooled in the preferred stance, but once they are at the top, they are allowed the flexibility to choose one of the other standard positioning styles.

A bugaboo with some modern catchers is the placing of a plate umpire's hand(s) lightly on the catcher's back when both are bending into their respective crouches, a ploy that Bauzá and instructors tolerate, as long as it is momentary. "This is used to gain balance," he explained. Because the umpire also is holding a small "clicker" between the left thumb and forefinger that tracks balls, strikes, outs and innings, what he is actually touching the catcher with on the left hand are only the three remaining digits.

Also required for the guy behind home plate are elaborate, hard-plastic shin guards, protecting the legs from knee-tops to the foot arches, and tucked easily inside gray, baggy "plate pants"; a bit higher in the anatomy, the hard-plastic "cup jock," its insertion transforming an ordinary cloth athletic supporter into a life-saving device; black, highly shined steel-toed shoes topped by a hard-shell exterior tongue attached to the footwear above the laces; a large, cloth bag (two bags are most popular these days, either in navy blue or gray) to hold baseballs, and attached by loops to the umpire's black leather belt; and a small brush, with firm bristles, to dust off the plate which fits neatly into either the back pants pocket, tucked into a small pocket inside the ball bags, or maybe a blue shirt pocket. A few plate umpires simply will wheel around to the non-pointed front of the "dish," kicking off dirt with a couple of swipes of their feet – thereby never removing brush from pocket.

Another set of tidbits about the necessary plate gear centers around the metal-and-padding protective mask, ribbed with thin, steel criss-crossing vertical and horizontal bars, with a protruding, U-shaped throat guard extending from the mask bottom. Like stances, there are differing schools regarding the mask's material composition. In one camp are those who prefer black rubber covering internal, foam-rubber padding to protect the chin and forehead. Others lean toward substituting soft, beige deerskin for the older rubber rendition. Gradually, a few umpires have experimented with a heavy-plastic helmet – dubbed The Tube because of the shape it resembles, fitting tightly to cover the head and the front part of the neck. However, the new equipment device, which vaguely replicates the headgear worn by hockey goaltenders, has a negative "sweet spot" in the vulnerable areas on both sides of the neck, from below the chin and jawbones down to the top of the shoulders (which will be discussed more in depth, in conjunction with a specific incidence, in Chapter 6).

As an adjunct to the small throat guard, some umpires – and many MLB catchers, and hockey and lacrosse goaltenders – enjoy enhanced personal safety by tying a hard-plastic, scoop-shaped attachment, known as a "Yeager," to the bottom of their masks. The implement derived its named from longtime Los Angeles Dodgers' catcher Steve Yeager (pronounced YAY-guhr), who also is coincidentally a distant cousin of famous pioneer test pilot Chuck Yeager. The first Yeager protector was personally designed for Steve Yeager, and later patented, by team trainer Bill Buhler in 1976 after Yeager's neck and esophagus were injured, as he knelt in the on-deck circle when a jagged piece of wood from teammate Bill Russell's shattered bat caromed at him.

On the bases, there are numerous recommended stances, positioning and rotations – varying greatly on each play and dependent on whether the "sacks" are empty, or how many bases are occupied. The three base umpires move in concert with their plate mate on plays with more than one base-runner, putting in motion the clock-like assortment of circular rotations to ensure total field coverage.

While the common public perception – including that widely subscribed to by some ill-informed broadcasters or overly judgmental sportswriters – on a blown call is that an umpire was "out of position," anyone who has umpired baseball at any level from Little League up to The Bigs will tell you *angle* is much more critical than *position*. To illustrate further, professional umpire schools often practice a drill whereby two student arbiters are stationed to make a "bang-bang" call at first base – one within only 10 feet or less from the base, but with vision obstructed; the other far out on the right-field warning track, yet with a perfect, unobstructed angle. Statistically, the distant outfield umpire gets the safe-or-out call correct more often than his "in position" counterpart because of all-important *angle*.

Having devoted four decades of his life to the umpiring profession – first as a minor league official, then 25 years as an AL arbiter, three years as an umpire consultant and finally six years as an MLB supervisor – Rich Garcia is keenly aware of what is required, body placement-wise, for any Man in Blue to succeed.

"Especially on a force play" – such as the "front end" of a potential double play at second base, with a runner who had been at first base, typically sliding aggressively to rattle the shortstop or second baseman – "it's extremely important to have that angle to put you into position to make that crossover step" and follow the ball from the middle infielder's throw to complete the "back end" at first base, he said. That maneuver involves the base umpire, in mid-infield between the pitcher's mound and second base, making a safe, out, (runner-generated) interference or (fielder-caused) obstruction call and spinning toward the first-base look with his left leg swinging to "cross over" his right as he completes a pivot.

"This is one of the first things I used to teach base umpires because it's so fundamentally important," Garcia emphasized in a series of interviews specifically for this book from December 2015 through May 2016. "Even though the guy at second base usually isn't (in a four-man crew) the one making the call at first," he added, *that* umpire is in that spot either to re-affirm, or suggest overturning, the decision of his colleague at first base, should there be a dispute by either team.

In the minors below the AAA level, there are typically two-man crews during the regular season, with partners traveling together from game to game in one of their privately owned vehicles, being reimbursed for gas mileage. While on the field officiating an actual game, that pair's "mechanics," which dictate their every move, also involve rotating to cover *every* base in *every* situation, **NEVER** losing track of the ball. Garcia termed this activity as "running their butts off, but doing it in a smart way." In this game, the *ball's* location/status always is the key determining factor on each pitch and its ultimate decision – based either on rules or umpire judgment.

Regarding the customary MLB four-man crews – which expand to six in the postseason to cover both the left- and right-field lines thoroughly – Garcia, in his inherent role as teacher, subscribed to what he termed "my *mantra.*"

"You're only as good as your No. 4 guy," he said. "So I always tried to make the No. 4 guy as good as everybody else" on a Garcia-led crew. The native of the Florida Keys also "made it a point to get along good with everybody, because I wanted to have the best crew."

Working together daily for six months a year, "you have to be happy" with your colleagues in a foursome, Garcia added. In his later years as one of nine MLB umpire supervisors in the first part of the 21st century, he said that, if dissent among umpiring personalities was detected, an otherwise competent individual was consequently shifted to another crew.

***

Back to the unnamed Latino-descent MLB umpire with the culinary expertise, that food fanatic chimed in by expressing bemusement with the cinematic depiction of his on-field profession – which always tends to incorporate more a movie director's fantasy vision of the ball-and-strike trade rather than ball yard reality. In fact, it seems, many filmmakers appear to be living in the '50s or '60s in their interpretation and portrayal of umpires.

"It's a joke among a lot of us how they depict umpires on TV and in movies," he lamented, again with that sly grin betraying an internal distaste for stereotypes – this time a tacit protest against a typecast more of an occupational, rather than ethnic, nature. "The balloon protector went the way of the buffalo a long time ago. But, you know, nearly every time an umpire is shown, he has the balloon.

"Not only that but it really irks me to see the buffoons they cast as plate umpires wearing backward caps under their mask – very unprofessional and very untrue," the anonymous MLB umpire said. The hats umpires wear underneath their previously described masks (an exception is The Tube, with no room inside for a hat) are custom-designed for a tight yet comfortable fit – staying neatly in place when a wearer briskly yanks the mask from his head to better assess a ball in play.

At least two former longtime Latino umpiring veterans – one in the majors, the other in the minors – concurred on the best on-screen presentation of their trade. The former was biased, of course, since he played an umpire in the movie, so he carries a Screen Actors Guild Card – just in case another Hollywood talent scout shows up and needs a genuine, SAG-ready umpire for the next baseball blockbuster.

On-field retiree Garcia was "assigned" first base in Director Sam Raimi's 1999 feature, *For Love of the Game*, often incorrectly referred to as *For the Love of the Game*. Other than having to shoot many scenes over-and-over, Garcia praised Raimi for his zeal in creating an authentic baseball experience for audiences.

MiLB executive Bauzá, who called games in the minors for nine seasons, said: "The most accurate movie, so far as showing real umpires as they are, is

For Love of the Game." He also surmised that those who make movies would be well served by recruiting *real* umpires – "guys like a Richie Garcia" – as technical advisors for their projects.

***

As of 2016, the updated MLB complement of Latino-ancestry regular umpires included the following multi-year veterans:

- **Angel Hernández**, 55, a Havana native who grew up in Florida and broke in as an NL fill-in (officially known as a "call-up") umpire in 1991, becoming full-time two years later;

- **Lazaro Antonio "Laz" Díaz, Sr.**, 53, also of Cuban descent but black and born and raised in Miami, Fla., who worked one season solely as a regular AL umpire in 1999 after getting a quick taste of the big leagues in 1995;

- **Alfonso "Fonzy" Marquez**, 44, the first Mexican-born MLB umpire who debuted as a full-time, exclusively NL umpire in 1999, and who has lived in Southern California most of his life but now resides in Arizona; he spent a gut-wrenching, nearly flawless 12 innings behind the plate in the deciding, fifth game of the 2015 World Series won by the Kansas City Royals over the New York Mets;

- **Manuel Augusto "Manny" Gonzalez**, 36, a native of Venezuela and five-year MLB veteran who is the first *Venezolano* to become an MLB umpire; the AL Wild Card game in 2015 marked his first postseason assignment.

Following their rookie seasons in 1999, Marquez in the NL, and Díaz in the AL, were transformed – with the entire *cadre* – into full-fledged MLB arbiters (*árbitros en español*). The major leagues, or *Las Grandes Ligas* in Spanish vernacular, underwent the umpire unification into a single entity whereby both leagues would be served by one group of on-field officials.

***

Two other umpires of Mexican ancestry – Angel Hernández Campos (no relation to veteran Cuban-American umpire Angel Hernández) and Ramon Armendariz, both California-born, with each standing about 5-foot-9 or 5-10 and weighing between 190-195 pounds – have worked in the major leagues, Campos to a much greater degree. However, both eventually were released after having followed Marquez as the second and third Mexican-descent MLB umpires but have continued to ply the trade at varying levels, including the two Class AAA minor leagues, collegiate conferences and even internationally – Taiwan, in Armendariz's case.

Campos was 33 when he made his MLB debut on May 3, 2007, in an AL interdivision game at Arlington's Globe Life Park (the name of the previous Ameriquest Field since 1994; it originally was simply called The Ballpark at Arlington) pitting the host Texas Rangers against the New York Yankees; he was assigned third base, with two salty old veterans, since-retired fellow Californian Derryl Cousins and Dana De Muth, joining him to patrol the bases, and Doug Eddings at home plate. (Eddings owns 88 Ump Irish Grill in Las Cruces, N. Mex., just an 88 mph "edible" slider away from his alma mater, New Mexico State University.)

Campos went on to work a total of 473 games over almost eight full seasons until his release at the end of the 2014 season. He made his U.S. minor league officiating debut in the Class A California League in 2000.

Armendariz, now 43 and a year older than Campos, logged several seasons in the Venezuelan winter leagues and in the Triple-A Pacific Coast League (PCL), earning more than a mere big league "cup of coffee" – probably more resembling a coffee *urn* – in 61 games from 2004-2007. His career in the minors began in 1995 at the relatively young age of 22.

***

After Armando Rodriguez and Rich Garcia blazed the path for Latinos in the majors, the one umpire who preceded all others as a minor league *Blue Hombre* was a current, 52-year-old Anaheim (Calif.) Police Department polygraph expert named Vincent "Vince" Delgado – we would not lie to you. Truth be told, though, Delgado, who back then was better known as Vinny, was cruising along exactly a quarter-century ago calling a game in the minors when a ball hit him in the head, and a resultant concussion ended his umpiring aspirations at age 25. It was the third time in five minor league seasons that he suffered a serious head shot from a ball tipped off a bat. Today, in addition to being a respected polygraph examiner throughout Orange County and surrounding Southern California, Delgado moonlights as an MLB Resident Security Agent at Angel Stadium of Anaheim, a ground-rule double (or two miles, actually) down the street from police headquarters.

***

At the end of 2015, there were other umpires with Latino backgrounds, one as old as 37, some in their 20s but most in their early 30s, already having worked major league games as call-ups for regulars who either were injured, on vacation or absent for other reasons deemed legitimate by their superiors.

They are technically employed by Minor League Baseball, which merged several years ago with the Professional Baseball Umpire Corp. (PBUC). Eventual major league umpires graduate mostly either from the official school formally known as the MiLB Umpire Academy, or a major and minor league-endorsed umpire school founded by the late former big league umpire Harry Wendelstedt, who died in March 2012. Wendelstedt re-framed the teaching curriculum and his campus's physical nature after buying the business in 1977 from retired major league umpire Al Somers. Both schools, conducted during baseball's off-season in January, are in Florida. The Wendelstedt entity is operated by his son, Hunter, an MLB umpiring veteran and non-Latino who was assigned to the 2015 AL Championship Series on the same six-man crew as Laz Díaz.

Similar umpire schools – some still operating and often owned by ex-big league arbiters – have come and gone over the years, producing some of the current older MLB crew members, but the academy and Wendelstedt are the two surviving officially sanctioned entities.

Several other contemporary Latino umpires have logged time as occasional substitute big league umpires – some during the regular season, others in spring training games either in Arizona's Cactus League or Florida's

Grapefruit League. There also is an Arizona Fall League, created by MLB front-office legend Roland Hemond, catering mostly to Triple-A umpires, or those about to move up to the AAA realm. That confederation of six teams, all in in the greater Phoenix area, utilizes the spring training facilities of a half-dozen major league organizations; it affords promising umpires an opportunity to hone their craft officiating games with players roughly from the same level.

Among the select group having been chosen as call-ups at one time or another were:

- **Gabe Morales**, 32, a Livermore, Calif., resident who made his MLB debut in 2014 but worked most of that year's regular season and 2015 in the Class AAA Pacific Coast League (PCL), the highest umpire proving ground for MLB in the West and Midwest, after umpiring MLB spring training games. (The International League is the Triple-A circuit on the East Coast);

- **Carlos Torres**, 37, the aforementioned Venezuelan debuted in the big leagues in 2015 after two seasons in the International League, following countryman Manny Gonzalez. However, Torres had served only call-up duty at the highest level during regular-season play while, like Morales, also having worked 2015 spring training until both Torres and Morales began the 2016 season on MLB crews; both, though, were on their respective crews in the new season technically as call-ups;

- **Ramon de Jesus**, 32, a 2014-15 PCL veteran and Dominican Republic native, similar to Laz Díaz in being both black and Latino, and although not having begun the 2016 season in the majors, he made his call-up debut the first month, on April 22 in Detroit; like Torres and Morales, he stayed in The Bigs well into summer 2016 – all being sized-up by seasoned crew chiefs on various four-man combinations, and each earning high praise and wide peer respect;

- **Chris Gonzalez**, 32, Campbell, Calif., who worked both the AA Texas League and PCL in 2014-15, and is not related to Manny Gonzalez;

- **Alex Ortiz**, 30, Los Angeles, Calif., who was on the 2014-15 PCL roster, and worked home plate in the internationally televised Triple-A All-Star Game (PCL vs. International League) at Omaha, Neb., in July 2015;

- **Roberto Ortiz**, 32, a Puerto Rico native who resides in Kentucky, a 2014-15 PCL operative, and no relation to Alex;

- **Albert Ruiz**, 29, an El Paso, Tex., native who lives in Las Vegas, Nev., and broke in as a PCL umpire in 2015.

Third and fourth Venezuelans, 35-year-old Jorge Terán and 33-year-old Robert Moreno, followed Manny Gonzalez and Carlos Torres into the profession, and were listed as being assigned in 2014-15, respectively, to the AA Eastern League and AAA International League.

Other Latino umpires employed by MiLB in various minor leagues in 2014-15 – and therefore edging closer to a collective goal of working permanently at the MLB level – were:

- **AA Eastern League** – Charlie Ramos, 27, Marshall, Minn., who worked the Class A Florida State League in 2014;

- **AA Southern League** – David Arrieta Quintero, Venezuela; and Jose Rafael Esteras, 35, Fort Lauderdale, Fla.;

- **AA Texas League** – Nestor Ceja, 29, Arleta, Calif., a current instructor at the MiLB academy in the off-season, and Ramon Hernández, also 29, Columbia, Mo.;

- **A-Advanced California League** – Adrian Gonzalez, Tucson, Ariz.;

- **A-Advanced Florida State League** – Derek Gonzales, 22, Orem, Utah;

- **A South Atlantic League** – Edwin Moscoso, Venezuela; Jonathan Parra-Valencia, Venezuela; and Alexis Trujillo, Stockton, Calif.;

- **A Midwest League** – Arturo Gonzalez, Norwalk, Calif.; Jesse Orozco, Peoria, Ariz.; and JC Velez-Morales, San Juan, P.R;

- **A Appalachian League** – José Navas Corzo, Venezuela, who was named the league's umpire of the year in 2015 and, mirroring Díaz and de Jesus, is Latino and black;

- **Short A NY-Penn League** – David Martinez, 33, Palm Beach County, Fla.; Anthony Perez, Murrells Inlet, S. Car.; and Jose Matamoros, 25, Waupun, Wis.;

- **Short A Northwest League** – Jesus Gonzalez, Tucson, Ariz.;

- **Rookie Advanced Pioneer League** – Californians Ricardo Estrada, Menifee; and Luis Hernandez, Lennox;

- **Rookie Gulf Coast League** – Navas Corzo and two other fellow Venezuelans, Emil Jiménez Pernalete, and Raúl Moreno Benitez. (Ages were undetermined for those listed as such. Also, as best can be determined, none of the various umpires either with surnames Gonzalez or Gonzales are related to one another.)

Terán, Robert Moreno and Arrieta also serve as *jefes de cuartetas*, literally quartet, or crew, chiefs, over three of the four *grupos* (groups of four-umpire-each instructor *cadres*) at home in the winter during the Venezuela Umpire Camp. The annual camp's other group *jefe* is Jairo Martinez, 43, the country's most experienced professional umpire with 19 seasons as an arbiter. However, most of that has been in South America and the Caribbean, except for a short stint several years ago in the International League.

***

Starting salaries for Major League Baseball umpires as of the 2015 season ranged from $84,000 to $300,000 for a 162-game regular schedule, depending on time of service, with extra pay incentives for working league postseason games. The salary is supplemented by a $340-a-day – *per diem* – allowance, which covers such essentials as hotel stays, car rental, meals and tips.

The umpires are entitled to four weeks' paid vacation during each regular season, with requests needing approval before the season begins. Three of the four weeks must be taken consecutively, the fourth at the individual umpire's personal discretion upon approval.

Vacation periods offer minor league umpires the opportunity for call-up assignments and increased exposure to larger crowds "under the Big Top." Coupled with vacation time, almost every regular who stays healthy winds up working somewhere between 130 and 140 games a season, not counting the postseason.

The odds of being a call-up are long, even for a competent, promising young umpire who has completed umpire school, and has worked an average of 5-7 years in the minors. According to MLB statistics, roughly 15-17 Triple-A umpires are called up annually.

A full-time, first-year MLB umpire conceivably can earn up to $120,000 that "rookie" season, depending upon depth of one's minor league experience.

Monthly salaries for MiLB-employed umpires in 2015 ranged from $2,600-3,500 in Class AAA, to $2,300-2,700 in Class AA, $2,000-2,400 in Class A Full Season, and $1,900-2,100 in Class A Short Season and Rookie.

Because many current umpires of Latino descent came either from U.S. *barrios*, or abject poverty in some Central or South American, or Caribbean, countries, the salary schedule, even in the lowest minor league, is regarded as a substantial step up, economically. The *material* compensation is almost *immaterial*, though, because, like professional umpires of *any* ethnic or socio-economic background, *Blue Hombres* typically regard their presence on MLB and MiLB baseball diamonds as a pleasure and well-earned privilege rather than purely as a paid pursuit.

Minimal requirements to be considered for an umpire position at any level of professional baseball, regardless of country of origin, include:

- High school diploma or GED;
- Reasonable body weight;
- 20/20 vision (with or without glasses or contact lenses);

- Reasonable English-speaking ability, with potential for improvement (as with body weight, "reasonable" is a largely subjective factor, determined case-by-case);
- Strong interpersonal skills;
- Good communication skills;
- Quick reflexes and good coordination;
- Some athletic ability;
- Required preliminary training for the job (i.e., professional umpire school).

1

ARMANDO RODRIGUEZ
WHATEVER BOWIE WANTS, BOWIE GETS

It was inevitable. Times were changing quickly, as the Vietnam War wound down and so-called Affirmative Action was starting to heat up in the mid-'70s. Baseball, America's sport, was gradually in danger of being replaced as the National Pastime by professional football, with the National Football League having merged with the much younger, but equally ambitious, American Football League less than a decade earlier.

At its highest level, the diamond pursuit still was separated into two distinctly different entities, in terms of personality and *modus operandi*. Until 1973, the older of baseball's two leagues, the National (NL), seemed a bit more modern, while the American (AL), nicknamed the Junior Circuit, was riddled with some old-fashioned habits. That year, a drastic change occurred when the younger league introduced the Designated Hitter (DH), yet the NL stood pat. Today, NL teams utilize the DH – a non-position player who only bats, typically for the pitcher – solely when visiting AL stadiums.

Even with their contrasting operational patterns, headed by strong league presidents, the NL and AL nonetheless were overseen by an individual above each league's top boss – the Commissioner of Baseball. At the time, that position was occupied by an iron-willed, bespectacled, Ivy League-educated lawyer from the Washington, D.C., area, Bowie Kent Kuhn. He was a Princeton University Economics graduate and alumnus of the prestigious University of Virginia School of Law. Kuhn became the sport's fifth commissioner in 1969, a year after team owners had forced the resignation of William Eckert, a retired Air Force officer who, whether a correct assessment, was widely perceived as incompetent in his three years on the job.

Kuhn had served for 20 years, immediately preceding his election by Major League Baseball (MLB) owners, as their legal counsel. Therefore, it seemed owners were basically giving him *carte blanche* to implement wholesale changes that, over the long term, would alter the face of American baseball forever. And with what amounted to a giant wrecking ball at his disposal, the imposing, 6-foot-5, 240-pounder (still the tallest and heaviest baseball commissioner in history) donned his figurative hard hat and pressed the "On" button to unleash the enormous metal orb onto the façade of the horsehide variety.

High on the ambitious Kuhn's to-do list was a racial evolution – or *revolution*, depending on whom you ask – akin to that which the sport had experienced in 1947 when player Jackie Robinson broke baseball's color line as the first black major-leaguer with the NL's Brooklyn Dodgers. Later the same year, another second baseman like Robinson named Larry Doby became the AL's first black position player, signing with the Cleveland Indians. Doby was joined soon thereafter by the first black pitcher, the ageless Leroy "Satchel" Paige, a Negro League legend.

The first black umpire in the majors was Robinson's fellow Southern Californian, Emmett Ashford, in 1966. He retired after five seasons.

As for Bowie Kuhn, though, he had an expanded vision – further integrate the leagues' separate umpiring complements. But this time he actively sought out a qualified "guinea pig," or "lab rat," as the first-ever MLB on-field arbiter of Latino ancestry. The earmarked man, yet-to-be-selected, would begin his hopefully long career in the next season – 1974 – exclusively in the American League.

Rich Garcia, who a year later would become the "Larry Doby" of baseball officials as the second Latino umpire, also in the AL, came *that* close to being the initial selection for the major leagues' version of a social science undertaking. However, a series of events revolving around him and Dick Butler, who was then supervisor of umpires, precluded the filling of that role by Garcia, by then a four-year veteran of calling balls and strikes in the minors.

At the time, at least according to one former knowledgeable insider, who declined to be quoted for this book in that regard, a suggestion by former

Cleveland Indians' star infielder and AL batting champion Bobby Ávila, aka "Beto" to Spanish-speaking fans, may have helped encourage Kuhn's eventual specific choice. The unnamed source intimated that then-Mexican League President Ávila strongly urged AL counterpart and close friend Joe Cronin to lobby Kuhn to select Cuban-born Armando H. "Mando" Rodriguez to be the Latino pioneer. Cronin was former field manager and general manager of the rival Boston Red Sox, for whom Ávila also played his final season in 1959. Rodriguez was familiar to the ex-Tribe star, having umpired in the Mexican League, a Triple-A-level entity south of the border whose teams had no direct working agreement with any major league clubs.

Garcia (who, incidentally, is not the unnamed source) vividly recalled, from a first-hand vantage point, how Rodriguez wound up as the initial full-time trailblazer for Latino MLB umpires.

Rodriguez, officially listed as 46 years old and resultantly far older than the average rookie in his AL role, had escaped a seaport city called Matanzas in his Communist island homeland. The 6-foot, 195-pound Rodriguez landed in South Florida in his 20s after Fidel Castro's regime seized control for good on New Year's Day 1959. (Garcia, himself a third-generation Floridian of Cuban descent, did speculate, however, that, while having no solid evidence to prove otherwise, he firmly believed Rodriguez was actually in his 50s when he became Kuhn's hand-picked Latino experiment subject.)

In addition to umpiring in Ávila's league, Rodriguez had worked amateur baseball around Miami and Fort Lauderdale. Prior to fleeing Cuba, he had been an experienced umpire on the Caribbean's largest island, where baseball has been a staple since the 1870s – almost as old as the game was in the United States. According to author Roberto González Echevarría in his 1999 book, *The Pride of Havana: A History of Cuban Baseball*, the sport, although mostly segregated with separate leagues for blacks and whites, was fairly free of government intrusion. After 1960, it morphed into a series of social experiments under Castro, as opposed to its more free-wheeling version under his predecessor, Gen. Fulgencio Batista, a fascistic-style dictator deposed by the bearded Communist revolutionary.

Rich Garcia, whose great-grandparents migrated with their small children from Cuba to Key West, Fla., shared an anecdote that underscored both the rock-hard enforcer and quick-tempered guy who was Mando Rodriguez. But Garcia also offered evidence as to why the Matanzas product had such a short-lived career as the first *Blue Hombre*.

"I worked with Armando my first year in the big leagues," said Garcia, now 73, but whose rookie AL season – the first of 25 – was Rodriguez's second, and final, "rodeo" ride under the MLB Big Top. "In the winter leagues in Cuba once, he had hit (MLB journeyman left-handed pitcher) Danny McDevitt with his mask," using the implement as a weapon, Garcia added when interviewed exclusively for this book. McDevitt, a five-year big-leaguer with four franchises, three in the AL, was the starting pitcher for Brooklyn, his only NL club, in the Dodgers' final game at Ebbets Field in 1958 before the organization permanently relocated to Los Angeles, according to his belated, Nov. 24, 2010, *New York Times* obituary, nearly a month following his death.

In Rodriguez's inaugural, Latino-groundbreaking AL season, he worked 159 games – the same amount he would log in his farewell campaign in 1975, in unofficial statistics compiled under the title of *The Baseball Cube*, an independent website operated by a Canadian baseball *aficionado* named Gary Cohen, who lives in a Montreal, Quebec, suburb. (Cohen's research is so intense – as is his zeal for accuracy – that official researchers at the Society for American Baseball Research (SABR) and Baseball-Reference.com rely religiously on his contributions, and those of a small handful of other totally dedicated "Horsehide Historians" like him.)

Even though it was not planned that way, Arlington, Texas, provided both an entry and exit site for Rodriguez's brief umpiring adventure in The Show. In the 40 (or 50?)-something Cuban's initial big-league game on April 4, 1974, he was assigned third base in a 7-2 win by the Oakland Athletics over the host Texas Rangers at now-defunct Arlington Stadium.

The rest of his crew included veterans Bill Haller behind the plate, Bill Kunkel at first and Merle Anthony at second. Outside of the novelty of Rodriguez's debut, other interesting trivia about the crew included: Haller was older brother of a contemporary MLB catcher, the late Tom Haller, who died in 2004 at age 67; the late Kunkel, himself a former big league relief pitcher, was the father of future Rangers' shortstop Jeff Kunkel; and the late

Anthony was an ex-minor league player. The elder Kunkel passed away in 1984 when he was only 48. Anthony was 67 at his death in 1993.

Crew Chief Haller also would figure prominently in almost-melodramatic events surrounding Rodriguez and his ill-fated departure in October 1975.

Yet, nearly two years previously, how Rodriguez was blended into the mix was intriguing from the get-go.

"Bowie Kuhn pushed getting Latin (American) umps. So they got Armando," Garcia remembered with a bit of reflective disappointment.

Nestor Chylak, with a reputation as a tough, decorated veteran of World War II's bloody Battle of the Bulge and a guy with the same kind of disjointed nose as ex-amateur boxer Garcia, momentarily transformed into a "locker room lawyer" defending his younger, promising partner in blue, Rich Garcia. The "judge and jury" in this impromptu, makeshift courtroom case was the baseball umpire supervisor, Butler. He had been dispatched obviously by Kuhn with a specific mission in mind. Said Garcia: "Nestor Chylak told Dick Butler, and pointing at me … he said, 'Why don't you hire him?' and Butler said, 'He's not ready,'" despite Garcia's four years of minor league seasoning coupled with working some big league spring training games.

Chylak, whose major league officiating career spanned from 1954-78, all in the AL, is one of only nine umpires enshrined in the Baseball Hall of Fame at Cooperstown, N.Y., and one of just two whose careers paralleled parts of Garcia's quarter-century tenure. The other Hall of Fame arbiter with on-field time concurrent with Garcia's is the NL's Doug Harvey, known jokingly as "God," for his tall stature, snow-white hair and aloof manner; he called balls and strikes in The Bigs for 31 seasons, from 1962-92. Chylak, who died in 1982, was inducted posthumously into the Hall in 1999, Harvey in 2010, both on votes by the Veterans Committee. Bill Klem and Tom Connolly were the first Hall of Fame umpire inductees, entering together in 1953.

***

Fast-forward almost two years to the 1975 season-ending series at the same Lone Star venue where Armando H. Rodriguez had called his first big league game a year ago the past April.

"We're ending our season in Texas, the second-to-last day of the season," Garcia said. "Bill Haller told me, 'You're gonna tell him (Rodriguez) he's not coming back.' I did the plate, took a shower, and Butler is there when I got out, and says, 'I think we're gonna tell him tonight.'

"So I'm crying the whole time. I had tears in my eyes when I told Armando" the bad news.

***

Bill Haller, who was to turn 81 in 2016 and living in the tiny historic village of Brownstown, 78 miles east of St. Louis, Mo., in his native Illinois, long after having retired from umpiring in 1982, was 6-foot-3½, a tad shorter than his younger brother, the catcher. With that imposing physical command, the older Haller carried the intelligence and articulate presence of a college professor, albeit one from the Old School, aka the University of Hard Knocks.

"Bill Haller was a good teacher. I learned a lot from him," Garcia said, an aura of awe in his voice. "He retired at 52 – way too early" in an era when many umpires remain on the job well into their 60s, or even 70s. While MLB recommends retirement by 65, it is not mandatory.

"My eyes … I couldn't judge the ball anymore," Haller conceded in a phone interview for this book in February 2016. "I couldn't stay, even though people were encouraging me to stay. The game's more important than anyone."

Haller went on to a single year as an umpire development supervisor, fired amid all the unexplainable intrigue of "office politics" at the top levels of all major sports. Nevertheless, despite many largely happy years as a longtime AL umpire and crew chief, the Illinoisan described his off-field position as "the best job I ever had in baseball," deriving satisfaction from watching his umpiring successors develop.

Haller's role models, ironically, were three highly placed big league executives who also were ultimately fired – former Commissioners A.B. "Happy" Chandler and Francis T. "Fay" Vincent, Jr., and former umpire Robert Calvin "Cal" Hubbard, who was umpire supervisor when Haller debuted in the majors in the 1950s. He was especially impressed by Hubbard, the only individual inducted into both the Baseball Hall of Fame and Pro Football Hall of Fame. Hubbard, who excelled as both a college and professional player, also is in the College Football Hall of Fame.

"Of all the baseball people I was ever around, Cal Hubbard was the best executive. He was brilliant, very intelligent," said Haller, who did a post-Korean War Army stint before becoming an umpire.

In another of life's ongoing ironies, Haller, a non-Latino but of Croatian bloodlines, does not speak Spanish, yet his brother, Tom, was fluent, working on improving his linguistic grasp beginning with a high school class in the basic tongue. Tom Haller contracted the West Nile virus, precipitated by a seemingly harmless, mosquito bite that caused brain damage, rendering him speechless and leading to his death several days later, when he owned a janitorial business in Indian Wells, Calif. With most of his employees of Mexican descent, his Spanish proficiency had been useful.

The flip-side of that bit of irony is brother Bill Haller wound up being the crew chief of a foursome that included MLB's first two *Blue Hombres*.

"I never considered it an insult when he asked me to take Armando under my wing," Garcia said, adding that he and Haller, eight years his senior, nonetheless shared a mutual respect as peers, and have remained good friends. That the former was the only crew mate who could converse with the Cuban *émigré* in Spanish was a bonus, and relief, for the savvy chief.

***

Back to the rest of the saga of the pacesetting MLB Latino umpires, for most of Rodriguez's final season, Garcia said Rodriguez was reluctant to speak much English, lest a player, coach or manager misunderstand him. Plus, "He refused to fill out" incident reports or any other necessary paperwork.

With these multiple problems besetting his new colleague and fellow Cuban-American, much of Rich Garcia's '75 season was spent on a four-man crew consisting of Crew Chief Haller, colorful half-umpire/half-comedian and future author Ron Luciano, soon-not-to-be-umpire Armando Rodriguez, and Garcia, a part-umpire/part-"baby-sitter" for a supposedly 47-year-old colleague. Luciano had *The Umpire Strikes Back* as the most popular of five books he authored during a 15-year period following his 1980 retirement from baseball. However, a complex personality, he took his own life in 1995.

"I worked on that crew mainly to help Armando speak English," said Garcia, who is conversant yet not fluent in the *idioma* of his ancestors. "What we spoke in Key West was kind of a slang Cuban" dialect. While his Spanish is less flowing than in his younger days, he admitted, "… but I understand and I still can conduct clinics" in such locales as Venezuela, with a relatively better-educated populace; the Dominican Republic, where reading proficiency generally is lower, and poverty prevails; and other countries throughout Latin America and the Caribbean.

He hopes he can somehow help discover the next Mando Rodriguez – only this time a younger prospect more willing *a prender inglés* (to learn English) … and fill out reports.

Spearheading the search – an Umpire Hunter, if you will – for future Latino MLB arbiters is a longtime former minor league umpire, Puerto Rico native and current South Florida resident Jorge Bauzá. He is a full-time employee of Minor League Baseball (MiLB); in addition to leading the way in devising Latin American recruitment strategies as Field Evaluator/Instructor, MiLB Umpire Development, and Lead Rules Instructor, MiLB Umpire Training Academy, Bauzá juggles several other important responsibilities tied in to umpiring specifically in the Caribbean region and generally the growing popularity of international baseball.

***

Armando "Mando" Rodriguez died in Miami, Fla., on Oct. 27, 2008, purportedly at age 79 (but perhaps much older, in the eyes of at least one former close colleague). Neither his widow nor known surviving family members could be located for interviews. It is believed he never umpired professionally again after 1975, but his pioneering place, both generally in baseball history and specifically as another chapter in overall Latino lore, is secure as the initial MLB *Blue Hombre*.

***

An added twist in the quest to be Major League Baseball's pioneer Latino umpire came in the person of Luis Benitez, a Cuban-American who resided somewhere in the Greater Miami-Dade Metropolitan Area.

Veteran umpire/consultant/umpire supervisor Rich Garcia has been affiliated with Major League Baseball or Minor League Baseball, without real time off except for vacations, nearly every day of his life, since 1970. Garcia is convinced that, with a break here or there, Benitez possessed the "right stuff" to have been the first Latino MLB umpire.

"He was one of my first partners in the Florida State League in 1970. Luis was an excellent umpire, but he had a (full-time) job, a wife and kids. So he couldn't take games except Miami and Fort Lauderdale," Garcia lamented.

Rich Garcia always is willing to talk about anybody but himself. However, he has his *own* compelling life story to share with anyone who asks.

2

RICH GARCIA

LEATHER NECK, THICKER SKIN

Earning respect does not come by accident; it is a long process at the end of which there lies a three-way junction of learning, growing and accommodating.

When entering unfamiliar territory, one first must strive to learn as much as possible about new surroundings.

Then, once familiarity has formed a firm foundation, seeds that become flowers continue to grow, even through cracks that have emerged in concrete.

Ultimately, the comfort associated with what has blossomed into the satisfying serenity of a peaceful place in life – colored by a palette of perennials – sets the stage for long-term harmony and tranquility.

Always combative like an ex-boxer or Marine – he's been both – Richard Raul Garcia nevertheless discovered this Zen-like trinity of life's lessons as a young umpire in the morass of professional baseball's lower minor leagues. For Rich, or even Richie, to many who knew him well enough to share parts of his inner *id*, the comparative level on baseball's food chain of the "deep bushes" to the major leagues was carp to caviar. As years progressed, he was forced to sample the bitter, salty aftertaste of the bottom-feeder but later savored the rich, scrumptious roe from Russian sturgeon.

Fresh from a four-year stint in the U.S. Marines, he followed that by earning a "plus" rating in umpire school, for which the talented middle infielder had spurned college baseball offers. After completing what was officially known as the Major League Umpire Specialization Course, Rich Garcia soon found himself getting "educated" in a novel manner, as he weaned himself away from the very streets that provided the backdrop for a few Hemingway novels. This one-time snot-nosed kid from the end of the necklace-like keys in Key West, Fla., southernmost city in the 48 contiguous states and last stop on the islet-hopping Intracoastal Highway, began trolling new turf in the Sunshine State's Lower Class A Florida State League (FSL). It still was a far cry from the hallowed ground of Yankee Stadium, Fenway Park and other fabled fields of dreams he would be patrolling for a quarter-century a few scant years later.

"Everyone's learning; you learn things – the players, the managers, the coaches, the umpires," admitted Garcia, who was newly married, 27, pushing 28, and pressing for precious exposure. His distant dream was to be a balls-and-strike caller someday in The Show, baseball's Broadway, Nirvana and Shangri-La all rolled into one. That goal eventually would be achieved, but first Garcia had to learn extreme patience and how to get along with some people – most of them at least four or five years younger than himself – who looked at him as a natural enemy.

The initial lesson for a tyro FSL umpire in any city at the edge of mangroves, marshes, and manatee and 'gator glades was perfecting the art of ejection – a kind of "launching," yet unlike those rockets not far away at Cape Canaveral. The colloquial term in UmpireSpeak is "tossing" an errant manager or ballplayer who either breaks some rule, blurts out a four-letter word, comments on a call by using a personal pronoun ("*You* missed that pitch!") or otherwise dares to challenge an umpire's proper authority to control the game's ebb and flow.

"Let's say you eject a player in 'A' ball," Garcia said as he began to paint a picture with his expressive hands. It was the same way his Cuban-born grandmother would do it just inside the entry way of the cozy little restaurant his parents owned on a side street, off busy W. Roosevelt Boulevard, near Naval Air Station Key West in the "Conch Republic" where he was born and grew up. "Then you see the same guy in Double-A, then Triple-A. It's about building relationships."

What Garcia was trying to illustrate was, despite an inherent adversarial co-existence, there is a reluctant, albeit prevailing, "semi-acceptance" – a co-dependency, if you will – in the two camps that one cannot exist without the other. Moreover, in each job, as participants on both the playing and officiating end advance, level by level, they inherently come to respect the other's specific role.

Consequently, Garcia learned early that, while a Marine had naturally grown into possessing a "leather" neck, it was more than handy for a baseball umpire to acquire, and maintain, a thick skin. When he reached the pinnacle of his profession, he perfected a certain psychological "gymnastic" – how to be civil and polite with players and managers without becoming a gushing fountain of over-friendliness.

"You can't get too buddy-buddy with players. You don't hold a nine-inning conversation," even with catchers, who crouch down right in front of you for nine or more innings, he said. "It can start problems with crews" and cause unnecessary animosity among umpires who must remain cool, calm, collected and completely in concert as they control the game. After all, having to live and work together for months at a time, each devises his own methods and magic to maintain a modicum of mental balance.

Once, in the early '90s, for instance, Garcia, the chief of his four-man complement, had a new, young umpire on his crew who went on to have a sterling officiating career. That particular spring day, though, had to be a turning point in the newbie's budding profession, as he found he was not "back on the block" anymore in the East Coast city where he lived all his life. He was on the opposite coast, being paid decent money to keep focused on a boy's game played by grown men as a means to support themselves and the families they rarely saw between February and November.

"I was working first base, and he was at second," Garcia reminisced. "Real early, I noticed that between every half-inning for the first three innings, he was carrying on a continuous conversation with the visiting shortstop, who he grew up with. He should've said, 'Hi, how ya' doin', once, then hustled his butt out to short center-field, where he could mind his own business and think about possible scenarios that might occur."

Garcia said it would have been acceptable, during the one- or two-minute breaks between half-innings, for his younger colleague to consult with *him*, the crew chief, or compare peer notes with a fellow newer umpire who was assigned third base. Either way, perhaps the chatty chap working second base might have picked up some subtle nuance he could use later in that game, or farther down the road in a tight, late September pennant race, where the outcome hinged on one of his calls.

"Finally, as soon as the third inning ended, I started to jog out to the rim between the first-base side of the infield where it meets the right-field grass," Garcia said. "As I moved, I caught the eye of my partner at second base and waved at him to meet me on the rim halfway between first and second.

"We only had a few seconds . . . but, without trying to use my hands like I usually do when I talk, I asked, 'You and (the unnamed shortstop) must know each other pretty well, huh?' My young partner says, 'Yeah, we go way back; we were altar boys together.' And I shoot back, winking and grinning while making a 'cutthroat' motion with my hand as I turned to go back to the first-base line, 'OK, no more fraternizing.' And that was that."

In the postgame umpires' room, Garcia was firm yet patient as he more thoroughly reiterated the boundaries of decorum to his two youngest crew members. He reminded them with a cautionary bent, while most players and managers saw only blue when looking at the arbiters, others always saw "red" – like in the "fire" of ongoing anger.

In just one illustration of that lesson, many years after his own MLB umpiring debut, Rich Garcia was confronted with an on-field situation at a much higher plane where any charitable aspects had virtually disappeared, and a major league umpire's elephant-like hide was tested.

***

Early July afternoons in Kansas City typically are hot, humid and what local TV meteorologists term susceptible to "the threat of late-afternoon thunderstorms."

However, on this particular Sunday – July 10, 1983 – the crowd of 37,565 at Royals (now Kauffman) Stadium probably was collectively wondering what happened to the so-called man-made "global cooling" that a national magazine had predicted four years earlier. As fans sat and sweltered in lower-90-degree heat, punctuated by a high dose of Show Me State humidity, it was even hotter and steamier on the playing surface, where the hometown Royals were primed to bat in the bottom of the first inning, striving to win the "rubber match" of a three-game series with their dreaded American League rivals, the New York Yankees. The only missing component was the usual midday storm in the ballpark on the Missouri side of the two-state metropolis most famous far and wide for its many barbecue restaurants.

Down on the field, in a routine he would eventually perform more than a thousand times in a big league baseball officiating career that spanned from 1975 to 1999, Rich Garcia watched the New York starting pitcher, southpaw Dave Fontenot, finish warm-up pitches, moved to the front of the plate to bend down and dust it off with his customized little, wooden-handled brush with the initials "RRG" carved into it, and then swung back around, standing behind home plate. He was waiting, as Yankees' catcher Rick Cerone returned from giving Fontenot last-minute instructions on the pitcher's mound and squatted down in front of him. KC's switch-hitting leadoff man Willie Wilson then entered the left side of the batter's box, digging in for a few seconds more to effect a comfortable stance, with Garcia, pointing toward Fontenot, hollering, "Play ball!"

In what would be a historical harbinger of an event two weeks in the future, the cocky, sarcastic Cerone, not one of Garcia's favorite catchers and a journeyman who also played for seven other big-league clubs between 1975-1992, already had begun antagonizing the veteran umpire, even before the warm-up tosses. All-Star third baseman George Brett, starting in right field that day and a left-handed hitter, was scheduled to bat third for the Royals, following Wilson and U.L. Washington.

Garcia recalled it, in an interview for this book in January 2016, as if the story had been yesterday: "Cerone, who I never had a good relationship with, comes out, and says, 'Hey, Richie, when Brett comes up, you're gonna call him out for too much pine tar on his bat.'

"I told him, 'You listen to me: I'm calling this game. You don't tell me what to do.' Brett's bat had pine tar most of the way up."

For the moment, though, a bit of the nervous edge was removed when Brett came to bat, going back to the bench quickly; he had popped out on a routine short fly ball on the first pitch. Garcia was relieved, noticing immediately that the back of Cerone's neck had turned beet-red from the anger still boiling inside the New York catcher, who likely would not pursue the issue, lest he be ejected.

Before the second inning began, Garcia quietly walked over to the Royals' dugout, intent on handling the situation proactively in *his* way. "I told (KC Manager) Dick Howser that if Brett came up again with *that* bat, I'd call him out," the plate umpire said. In Brett's subsequent at-bats, he used a "cleaner," legal bat.

"You know, there was no problem the rest of the way, so I was astounded at what happened a couple of weeks later in Yankee Stadium, and watched the highlights on TV – with the same two teams but a different umpiring crew," Garcia added.

He was referring to one of the most famous non-postseason brouhahas in baseball annals, on July 24, 1983 – forever known from that day forth as The Pine Tar Incident. The sport's tallest umpire at the time, 6-foot-6 Tim McClelland, was behind the plate when Brett, having reverted to his familiar bat rubbed with gooey pine tar beyond the acceptable point on the handle, stepped in to the batter's box in the top of the ninth inning; the future Hall-of-Famer slammed a home run to right field off the Pinstripes' star closer and eventual fellow Hall member, Rich "Goose" Gossage, to give the Royals the lead.

After Brett victoriously circled the bases and crossed home plate, crafty little Yankees' Manager Billy Martin emerged from the opposite side, gesticulating wildly in the manner of the tough little Italian/Portuguese-ancestry brawler from California's East Bay that he was, pointing angrily toward the visitors' dugout.

McClelland sauntered over to Howser, asking for Brett's mostly stained bat, then, as he returned toward home plate, waved it in the air with his left hand, while, with his other thumb in the air, called Brett out – nullifying the home run.

It is easy to log on to YouTube and watch the whole episode, as Brett "went bananas," charging McClelland, and earning an ejection. In intervening years, the controversial incident has gotten well over a half-million views.

Given what had transpired a fortnight earlier in Kansas City involving the same combatants, Garcia admitted, "I was astounded that, here are the same two teams and, after all that happened a few days earlier . . . this is taking place."

The old, long-standing "Pine Tar Rule" no longer exists, as such. MLB umpires do not allow use of pine tar, beyond the trademark, on wood bats – which the big leagues only use – to give batters a better grip. However, if an umpire *does* detect an indiscretion – or the opposing team calls his attention to it – there is no penalty on the batter, like being called out or ejected from a game; the bat is simply removed from play for the remainder of the game. Before the old rule was eliminated, pine tar was not allowed closer than 18 inches from the knob at the bottom of the bat handle; umpires regarded the 17-inch-wide home plate as a close-enough "ruler" to measure whether a bat was legit; and with the out/ejection possibilities still in the rulebook back then, the outcome hinged on whether the guilty batsman opted to go quietly back to the dugout or more vociferously vented displeasure the way Brett did.

At least one notable instance with pine tar resulting in ejection occurred on April 23, 2014, when a New York Yankees' pitcher was basically "up to his neck" in the gooey substance. In a game at Yankee Stadium III against bitter arch-rival Boston, non-Latino plate umpire Gerry Davis, a veteran crew chief who has worked with several *Blue Hombres* over his nearly four-decade big league career, gave New York's 6-foot-7 Michael Pineda the first-inning "heave-ho" when the right-hander was detected with gobs of pine tar rubbed on his neck. Perhaps the sticky stuff could have helped, as the Red Sox ultimately prevailed, 5-1.

***

Anyone who has "called ball" at the highest professional level for, say, at least five years easily can achieve status among wags and pundits as a bona fide "character." While most MLB umpires would much rather not have a spotlight shone on them, human nature being what it is, individual personalities often belie the desire for anonymity.

With this in mind, fitting the bill well was the quartet of baseball officials who gathered to work the Aug. 4, 1993, nighttime battle between the AL West leaders, Chicago's White Sox and Texas, at the Rangers' home ground, Arlington Stadium. (As of 2016, the latest, most cosmetically re-done, re-dubbed version of the ballpark-of-many-names at the same site was Globe Life Park.)

That was when perhaps the most talked-about on-field fisticuffs of the second half of the 20th century broke out, yet without the advance publicity of ring battles billed as the Fight of the Century. Rather than just a hockey-style, gloves-off tiff pairing a couple of ordinary, rag-tag journeymen, the bout matched one of the sport's best clutch hitters against whom many regard – if career wins (324), no-hitters (7) and strikeouts (5,714) count as extra credit – as the best right-handed pitcher ever.

Moreover, one of the on-field arbiters had a stint as a wrestling referee behind him, setting up an ideal scenario for a hardball fist fest.

Here's how a noted prizefight announcer like Michael Buffer might have put it (but naturally not until he had famously intoned his signature, deep-baritone introduction: *"Le-e-t's get read-y to r-r-rumbl-e-e-e!"*):

"In the White Corner, from Santa Maria, California, and weighing in at 185 pounds: Rob-b-in Ventura-a-a. In the Blue Corner, from Alvin, Texas, and weighing in at 195 pounds: No-lan Ry-a-n-n-n."

The American League umpiring crew assigned to officiate the teams' three-game series was arguably one of the diamond sport's most colorful, considering all the components of its human parts. It was helmed by Crew Chief Garcia, who was stationed at third base. Dale Ford, an AL umpire for 26 years whose final year also was 1999 and now is a Tennessee Republican State Representative, was behind home plate. Fifth-year operative Chuck Meriwether, only the fifth black AL umpire in history when he debuted in 1988 and the first since black door-opener Emmett Ashford's retirement in 1970, worked second base. However, hanging out down there at first base was eight-year veteran Larry Young. During a 1995 umpires' lockout, he had refereed a World Wrestling Federation match.

As crew chief, it was Garcia's duty, in pre-game preparations, to warn the other three of anything unusual that might be expected, particular trends that were germane, or reiteration of individual players' peculiarities. Because this was the second of a three-game series, the heads-up session would be shorter than the previous night's series opener. That first game had been a comparative yawner, with the visitors routing the Rangers, 11-6, chasing Texas starter Charlie Leibrandt by scoring nine runs in the first two innings, as Rich Garcia enjoyed the equivalent of a familiar Gulf Coast beach party behind the plate, getting done in under three hours, and not witnessing a single hit-batsman. He looked at a total of only 264 pitches between the two staffs, an average of less than 30 pitches in each full inning.

The next evening was somehow ominous, though, considering Nolan Ryan's presence, coupled with his history facing Chicago batters.

"I had heard that something had come up in the White Sox locker room, that they had made a pact to go after Ryan if he hit somebody," Garcia intimated when interviewed exclusively for this book, "so we had an idea something might happen, and were prepared if it did."

The savvy crew chief from the Sunshine State did not have to possess genie-like prescient powers, then, to predict "if," since it was just a matter of "when."

After Chicago had scored twice, one run on Robin Ventura's line-drive RBI single to left, staking the visitors to a quick lead in the top of the first inning, he came to bat with one out, the bases empty, in the top of the third, with the Sox still up, 2-0. Ryan wasted no time, plunking him in the left shoulder blade with the first offering, a "hello-I'm-here" fastball – as if the first-inning single instead had been a home run.

Therefore, what surprised Garcia and Co. was not the "rhubarb" itself, yet that normally clear-headed Chicago Manager Gene Lamont had allowed the usually docile (except when hitting – lifetime average of .257, but tied for fifth all-time with 18 grand slam home runs) future White Sox manager, Ventura, to be the earmarked attacker of Ryan. It was customary for the left-hand-hitting third baseman to be a sometimes Designated Hitter, *not* the Designated Enforcer.

"After Ryan hit him with a pitch, (Ryan) stayed around the mound, and Ventura seemed reluctant to do anything. He just headed down the line towards first base," with Ford following right behind to ensure safe passage, Garcia remembered. Then, about halfway up the 90-foot baseline, the Sox star suddenly turned and sprinted at Ryan, with both benches emptying and waves of Pinstripes and Lone Star-adorned young men flooding the circular rim of the pitcher's mound.

The Texas hurler, accustomed to "bulldogging" steers to the ground growing up on his family's South Texas ranch, slapped a quick and sure headlock on his attacker, proceeding to begin chopping at Ventura's face with a series of punches that probably were held back somewhat by the Rangers' ace.

All told, the fracas lasted less than a minute, as do most horsehide rhubarbs; Garcia, Ford and Meriwether – who retired years later and became an MLB umpire supervisor – joined "real" one-time referee Young in bringing peace. In fact, little (5-9) Richie is very visible in several images of the affair, right in the middle of trying to break in to extricate the 6-2, 195-pound Ryan from further potential harm by Ventura's teammates. Ironically, he got unexpected help from an occasional past target of the Texan's "chin-music heat," Chisox two-sport star Bo Jackson, also late of the NFL's Oakland Raiders.

As Ryan is seen having moved off to the first-base side of the mound, bending over trying to regain his breath, Garcia is alongside him, checking on his welfare, just like a good crew chief is expected to do.

"I was basically telling Ryan to keep his cool, and not to move from where he was at," Garcia said. "I told him he was staying in the game because he was just defending himself, but not to ruin it now."

In that leadership role, the latter already had ejected both Lamont and Ventura, partly for using the occasion to exact unnecessary revenge for events dating back two or three years. However, the primary reason for sending the two to the showers early was really more for what, in a real court, would have been "malice aforethought" charged to the current White Sox manager, and "instigating assault" on the part of the future Chicago skipper. The unexpected detour to the mound also netted Robin Ventura a two-game suspension.

The Hall of Fame right-hander completed seven full innings, combining for a four-hitter with relievers Craig Lefferts and Tom Henke, as the Rangers took the series, two-out-of-three, winning, 5-2, and scoring all their runs in the bottom of the sixth.

***

Fans being fans – and especially Orioles fans being from Baltimore – Rich Garcia may sit near the top of the list of individuals most hated by sports *aficionados* in Charm City, which is not charmed at all when the collective fandom there feels its team has been jobbed, to use as kind a euphemism as possible to capture the essence of the bad vibe if the O's, the NFL's Ravens or even the collegiate Maryland Terrapins (Terps, more familiarly) are done a perceived wrong.

Sports loyalists all along both shores of Chesapeake Bay, not just around Baltimore itself, are much like fans just to the northeast in rival Philadelphia. In Philly, not only do they boo their own professional teams when they have the kind of overall bad calendar year the local paid athletes suffered across-the-board in 2015, but they are reputed to "dis" Santa Claus and boo and hiss at planes taking off and landing at Philadelphia International Airport, not far from major sports venues. It might make you think of not-so-brotherly hate rather than Brotherly Love.

***

Even farther northeast, it is Oct. 9, 1996, back in the South Bronx long before Michael Pineda ever thought of pine tar as a good neck "medication":

Game One of the American League Championship Series at Yankee Stadium is progressing, with Garcia, a seasoned crew chief during the regular season, stationed down the line in right field, as the visiting Orioles lead the hated New Yorkers, 4-3, in the bottom of the eighth inning. The Pinstripes' captain, shortstop Derek Jeter, steps in with one out and the bases empty.

Baltimore relief pitcher Armando Benitez serves up the first pitch, which a zoned-in Jeter launches to the opposite field, the high fly ball heading toward the warning track in right, and maybe "outta here," as the Orioles' late, legendary play-by-play man, Chuck Thompson, might aptly have described it; it is going to be *that* close.

Tony Tarasco, having replaced starter Bobby Bonilla in right for defensive purposes and turning toward the fence on the crack of the bat, seemingly times his leap perfectly, his back braced against the wall. However, *"Where's the ball, dammit?"* he wonders, yet gets no satisfaction.

With his leap and "catch," Tarasco, who was born not far from the spot where the play is occurring and played for the Yankees three years later, assumes the ball is in the pocket of the glove ... only it is Jeffrey's glove. *"Who? What? Where?"* And before the quick right-fielder even has time to think, he instinctively looks down quickly at the reddish warning track, contrasting greatly with the green outfield wall, all the while trying frantically to locate the ball he thought he had caught.

In a split-second, conceding maybe the ball left the yard and eked into the first row of seats, Tarasco turns back disgustedly toward the infield and spots the umpire. Garcia is twirling his right wrist, forefinger extended, high above his head, signifying "home run" – much to the Orioles outfielder's disappointment, and pretty much that of everyone back in Baltimore and environs.

Oh, and Jeffrey? He's Jeffrey Maier, the 12-year-old New Jersey boy whose name – at least as far as hard-rock O's buffs are concerned – will go down in the Partisan Baseball Fans' Book of Infamy with Cubs fan Steve Bartman at Wrigley Field – equal in that warped sense to the Japanese bombers at Pearl Harbor. The ball Tony Tarasco cannot locate lands in the young lad's glove, having hit the pre-teen's arm first, as Maier has reached out over the top of the fence into the still-live field of play. Garcia's initial view in the "bang-bang" world of umpiring is that the youngster has indeed caught the ball, but behind the imaginary line dividing the field from the seats.

In a postgame story the next day, *The New York Times* reports: "Television replays clearly showed that without interference, the ball would have hit near the top of the fence or Tarasco would have caught it to put the Orioles four outs away from a 4-3 victory." Tarasco tells *The Times*: "Obviously, I was camped underneath it and ready to catch it."

The outcome results in the Yankees tying the game at 4-all, going on to win, 5-4, in 10 innings, and capturing the ALCS, 4-1. They advance to the World Series, defeating the Atlanta Braves in six games.

As for Rich Garcia, the fickle Baltimoreans will hold the call against him forever, even though the always stand-up guy admits after the game that he blew the call, which should have been ruled fan interference, making Jeter the second out instead.

"I never saw the ball hit (Maier's glove)," Garcia admits in a postgame interview.

"It has come to a point where it does not bother me," he said when asked (by a Baltimore newspaper columnist, of course, in a 2012 interview) about the play that Orioles' partisans will not let go away – even 16 years after it occurred. "It is part of baseball history; that is what baseball is all about. I have dealt with it. I have said what I have to say."

***

The funny thing about ever-enduring incidents is not necessarily the tragic effects but the sometimes pleasant, often conciliatory, *after*-effects.

For instance, long after their "meeting" at the mound in the Metroplex, Nolan Ryan and Robin Ventura made up, and it manifested itself into a mutually respectful relationship. Ryan, in his role as part-owner of the Rangers in his later years, heaped praise on Ventura for his "skipper style" as White Sox manager; and the former adversary, in turn, lauded the retired pitcher for *his* management "mojo."

Whether Tony Tarasco and Rich Garcia have forged a similar alliance is unknown. However, it might have been conceivable, given that both carry a bit of Hollywood inside of them.

In addition to the Orioles and Yankees, Tarasco played for four other big league teams – Atlanta, Montreal, Cincinnati and the New York Mets – as well as Japan's Hanshin Tigers, and was the Washington Nationals' first base coach for three seasons until he and the entire coaching staff were fired in a total "house-cleaning" following the 2015 season. However, with the wardrobe people having only a Kansas City Royals uniform available, he made a cameo appearance in a 1991 movie, *Talent for the Game*, a box office "bomb" that told the story of a major league scout. Although indeed a New York City native, Tarasco, whose cousin is MLB infielder Jimmy Rollins (who began 2016 with Robin Ventura's White Sox), moved as a youth with his family to Southern California, where he graduated from Santa Monica High.

Eight years after that film had gone quickly from theaters to video stores, Garcia, like Tarasco, found himself holding a Screen Actors Guild card, and mostly back at Yankee Stadium. The occasion was the filming of *For Love of the Game*, in which he was one of three real professional arbiters who portrayed umpires. The Floridian was assigned first base, joined by two since-retired, yet then-active, big league colleagues, Rick Reed on the plate and Jerry Crawford at second base. The fourth umpiring slot, covering third base, was filled by a non-umpire away from the movie shoot, Michael Bellisario, whose father, Donald P. Bellisario, has been one of network TV's most successful scriptwriters for decades.

Garcia landed the role, basically playing himself in a familiar setting, because former Cal State Fullerton coach Augie Garrido, a close pal who had since moved on as head coach of the Texas Longhorns, also was a good friend of actor Kevin Costner, who had attended the Fullerton, Calif., school.

Based on a novel by Michael Shaara, and directed by Sam Raimi, the two-hour, 17-minute presentation starred Costner and Kelly Preston. The story line was redemptive, chronicling the attempted comeback of a 40-year-old, over-the-hill pitcher, played by athletically inclined Costner, whose love interest was Preston, real-life wife of actor John Travolta. While the film was far more popular than *Talent for the Game*, which grossed only about $336,000, the $46.1 million it pulled in at the box office was short of the $50 million Raimi and his colleagues had budgeted for the project.

"I was sent a script, but I didn't read it," Garcia said. "I thought it was a baseball movie, but it was a love story."

The film took 31 days to shoot, in such diverse locations as Southern California, Colorado and in and around New York City.

Garcia and the three other cinematic umpires, though, had their work filmed predominantly at Yankee Stadium on a chillier-than expected evening – which was problematical.

"It was a cold night in the fall in New York City, and we had to wear short sleeves," he said, shaking his shoulders to simulate shivering.

Yet the chill became almost non-consequential, compared to a scene featuring actor John C. Reilly, playing Costner's long-time catching buddy. When his turn at bat came, Reilly was required to step in to the same batter's box as Derek Jeter, Bernie Williams and their Yankee teammates did at every home game in the spirit of Babe Ruth and Lou Gehrig, and take his cuts. But the fairly non-athletic actor, or physical antithesis to the muscular, sports-oriented Costner, was unable to capture any latter-day Bronx Bomber magic.

"We had a scene where John C. Reilly hits the ball into right field. (But) he's not an athlete," Garcia said, utilizing keen recall powers to capture the essence of a scene shot 17 years earlier. "He only has to touch the bat to the ball," to preserve the moment via digital technology, thus enabling transfer to a computer, which then would automatically attach the image to the end of the batted ball's path.

"He couldn't do it," on the first nine attempts – theoretically striking out the equivalent of three times in a single plate appearance – "but on the 10th swing, he finally did it," Garcia added, shaking his shoulders once more and breathing a sigh of relief that he was not out in the cold but merely *talking* about it this time.

***

Rich Garcia likely would be first in line at the window entering the Pearly Gates – the one where those who have reached the Hereafter are required to admit that "nobody is perfect." Yet, in light of that willingness to confess to *some* flaws, the man who called several thousand big league contests can say with confidence that he is one of only seven umpires in baseball history to have worked two perfect games by pitchers at the sport's highest level.

The two perfectos he officiated were thrown 17 years apart – first, by the Cleveland Indians' Len Barker, 3-0, over the Toronto Blue Jays on May 15, 1981, the other on May 17, 1998, by New York Yankees' southpaw David Wells, who skunked the Minnesota Twins, 4-0. Garcia was behind the plate for the Barker gem, and watched the Wells winner from third base.

"Barker was right on the money; he struck out 11 batters, and his catcher, Ron Hassey, not only made it easy for me on a cool night by calling a great game, but also had one of the RBIs, and we got out of there in just over two hours at the old Cleveland stadium," Garcia remembered in a January 2016 interview for this book, as if the game had been yesterday rather than 35 years ago. It was in same manner as his gift of recall of his role as a cinematic umpire. "The thing about it was, I don't think anyone really noticed." The AL umpire was referring to an almost non-existent crowd of about 7,000 fans, bunched together mostly in the lower deck in the cavernous ballpark for a game with sub-50-degree temperatures, chilly for mid-May, alongside always-windy Lake Erie, and likewise, shades of the Yankee Stadium "movie set" some years later.

"Actually, I'd never admit it then, being as neutral as possible, but I felt kind of sorry for the Toronto pitcher, a right-hander from Venezuela named Luis Leal. He also went the distance and gave up only one earned run – on a solo homer, I believe, by Jorge Orta, the muscular slugger from Mexico, in the bottom of the eighth," Garcia said, keeping that memory for descriptive, long-ago detail in overdrive. The Indians had posted a pair of unearned runs in the first to lead, 2-0, and never looked back, even though Leal shut them out from then until the eighth.

Like Barker on the earlier occasion, Wells struck out 11 Twins batsmen.

"Big Tim McClelland (all 6-foot-6 inches of him) was back there calling balls and strikes," said Garcia, who enjoyed the view from his little corner at third. Joining him on the bases were John Hirschbeck at first and Mike Reilly at second.

The following season, 1999, would be the last hurrah on the field for Richard Raul Garcia, as the labor turmoil turned baseball's calm, complacent pace topsy-turvy. He was among those who had threatened an all-out labor stoppage, then had resigned voluntarily but not one of those re-hired when the two leagues consolidated their umpires into a single working entity to start the New Millennium.

***

If one gathers that nothing earth-shattering shook Rich Garcia's on-field orbit early in the 1990s and even before then, the assumption would be incorrect.

Guess who was assigned to work the plate in the opening game of the Bay Bridge World Series on Oct. 14, 1989, matching cross-bay rivals the NL's San Francisco Giants against the favored AL champion hosts, the Oakland Athletics?

Answer: Why, Rich Garcia, of course, but more elaboration in a moment.

This ubiquitous figure had an unplanned penchant for being crouched behind opposing catchers in some of baseball's most noteworthy, or infamous, contests that generally form the fabric of modern baseball lore, and add spice – or maybe *salsa picante* – specifically to the legend of *Blue Hombres* and the undisputed spiritual leader of those Latino call-barkers. Ryan-Ventura, the Jeffrey Maier incident, the pair of perfect games – you name it.

In that regard, it was not surprising on April 12, 1992, back at Cleveland Municipal Stadium, there to witness yet another baseball oddity that belonged on the pages of *Ripley's Believe It or Not* was plate umpire/Crew Chief Rich Garcia. This time, it was an event, odds-wise, rarer than a perfect game – a complete-game no-hitter by a hurler, who was the *losing* pitcher.

However, heed this message from our sponsor, as we first travel back to 1989, to discuss more thoroughly, what has come to be known in final annals as "The Earthquake Series," Giants versus Athletics, in one of the world's most temblor-prone regions. The schedule had Oakland hosting the first two match-ups in the best-of-seven series on Oct. 14 and 15 at the Oakland Coliseum.

With Rich Garcia, who headed the six-man crew, selected to call balls and strikes, heavily favored Oakland, behind right-hander Dave Stewart's five-hit, complete-game gem, blanked the visitors, 5-0, on a dry, 65-degree evening. Stewart had flawless control and "command," striking out six, not issuing his only walk until the eighth inning, allowing a lone extra-base hit on Will Clark's line-drive double in the sixth, and inducing San Francisco batters into 10 ground-outs and eight routine pop-outs or fly-outs.

On the surface, it seemed like the continuation of a week-long, fairly peaceful gathering of bayside neighbors who did not necessarily like each other, yet tolerated one another enough to face off in a few friendly games of baseball. However, within less than two days, any semblance of a backyard barbecue would go up in *real* flames, literally shaking everyone to the earth's restless core, and triggering numerous large blazes which always result from major quakes.

Following that Saturday Series opener, the Athletics staked themselves to a 2-0 advantage, defeating the Giants, 5-1, with an identical profile to the evening before – same game length of about 2¾ hours, crowd size about 49,000 and dry weather in the mid-60s.

Then, after an off-day on Monday, the series had shifted eight miles across San Francisco Bay to already fragile Candlestick Park. The 30-year-old stadium – since demolished and replaced by modern AT&T Park, five miles north – was known to locals as "Candlestink," due to an unpleasant aroma from a nearby sewage treatment plant, coupled with smelly tidewater, blown into the aging venue by always-swirling gusts coming in right off the bay where the land jutted out into an incongruous point.

It was just past 5 p.m., Pacific time, on Tuesday, Oct. 18, a half-hour before the scheduled start of Game 3 in the best-of-seven competition. Accomplished ABC-TV play-by-play man Al Michaels, who tried to sum it up the way he had with the U.S. Olympic hockey "miracle" nine years earlier, was unable to finish the sentence before the telecast went black for a few minutes: *"I'll tell you what, we're having an earth-."* Then power suddenly was gone. The Loma Prieta quake, although centered 50 miles south of the World Series site, was 7.1 in magnitude on the Richter Scale, strong enough to collapse a major elevated freeway stretch across the water in Oakland. Worse yet for baseball adherents in the massive disaster that also triggered the aforementioned fires predominantly from broken gas lines, and took 42 lives, all over the Bay Area, was the initial tremor and aftershocks were causing concrete from Candlestick's upper deck to crumble like sugar cubes in a morning coffee cup.

"I had never been in an earthquake," admitted Florida flatlander Rich Garcia. In fact, he and all but one crew member – Canada-born but lifelong California resident Paul Runge – were mostly from the East Coast or the Midwest, in one case, so this surprise natural phenomenon was an unfamiliar, and freaky, occurrence. Runge, who lived in San Diego during most of his umpiring career, was part of the only family of three generations of major league umpires; he was preceded by his father, Ed, who was a National League arbiter from 1954-70, and followed by son, Brian, who worked as an MLB umpire from 1999-2012.

"We waited around (in the Bay Area) for three more days before the rest of the series was postponed for 10 days," Garcia said. "It was a scary experience, and I'm not *that* easy to scare. But I couldn't wait to fly home and take it easy for a few days." At the time, the umpires were not happy with their ultimate boss, Commissioner Fay Vincent, who had decided to postpone the first World Series of his tenure without immediately and first consulting the very people who were officiating the annual event.

By the time the umpires, and everyone else, had returned, the Athletics quickly completed a Series sweep with respective 13-7 and 9-2 victories in Friday and Saturday evening games at Candlestick. Garcia, normally unflappable and even-tempered unless provoked beyond reasonability, conceded that he was privately somewhat antsy all during Games 3 and 4, despite being respectively stationed down the left-field line and at third base – hoping all along that the San Andreas Fault would not re-awaken, like a slumbering, athletic giant on these two nights.

"What I had seen and experienced already, I didn't ever want any part of again," he said.

Two and a half years later on a sunny but chilly (41 degrees) Sunday in Cleveland, the stage was set for a doubleheader between the hometown Indians and Boston Red Sox. It was Rich Garcia's turn to do the plate again in the opener. Appropriately, then, this was an occasion in early spring to wear his navy blue, lined pullover windbreaker adorned with double vertical white stripes over each shoulder and bearing the familiar "19" – the longtime umpire's personal touch – embossed into the right sleeve, just below the shoulder. The jacket was amply sized to fit easily over his inside chest protector and turtleneck and powder blue short-sleeve shirt layers. He also kept a pair of gloves tucked into his ball bag, even though he probably would opt to leave them there.

The day was a bittersweet one for Boston starter Matt Young. The Red Sox left-hander could not exult in his performance; after all, he had pitched his only no-hitter. Problem was, he lost, 2-1, as the Tribe posted two unearned runs. The visitors avenged that in the nightcap, with Roger Clemens notching a 3-0 shutout.

In the first game, behind a five-hit outing by righty Charles Nagy, Cleveland scored one run each in the first and third innings to counteract a lone Boston marker in the top of the fourth, nine hits and, of course, Young's hitless pitching. The hosts parlayed a walk and consecutive steals of second and third by Kenny Lofton into the first-inning run when Bosox Hall of Fame third baseman Wade Boggs's throw, after fielding a Carlos Baerga grounder, sailed over Mo Vaughn's head at first. Then, in the bottom of the third, the no-hit Clevelanders' Mark Lewis scored via a one-out fielder's choice on another Baerga ground ball. That had followed back-to-back walks by Young issued to Lewis and Glenallen Hill, the slow-footed Hill's unlikely steal of second having pushed Lewis to third.

"I'd been around a long time, but I never had seen anything quite like that, a no-hit pitcher losing – even in the minors," an astonished Garcia said.

Because of the loss, the actual no-hitter went into the books as "unofficial."

***

Being regarded as somewhat of a baseball ambassador in his role as an umpire-emeritus, Garcia, who generally still is in good health for a septuagenarian, often is tapped to venture down to various Latin American venues for scouting or instructional purposes.

For instance, in his first of three years as a consultant to the Baseball Commissioner, Allan H. "Bud" Selig, and his initial year as a "civilian" following 25 major league seasons as a *Blue Hombre*, Garcia got the call.

"In the summer of 2000, Major League Baseball asked me to go to the Dominican Republic to upgrade some World League umps," Garcia recalled. "If you lived in a city, you were allowed to umpire … in your respective complex in the same town in which you resided. The stadiums were part of academies owned by certain MLB teams.

"I would evaluate," he added, harkening back to the hours upon hours of the horrid heat and humidity of Hispaniola, the island on which the Spanish-speaking country occupies the eastern half, with Francophile Haiti filling out the western flank. Garcia sat, clothes getting drenched with sweat, in an inflexible, hard-plastic stadium seat, taking notes similar to a scout. His ink began to "run" and smudge, in the searing subtropical climate; it was literally the polar opposite of his frigid film shoot in Yankee Stadium the previous year.

"Then," he said, not successful in trying to hide an evil grin, "I would *run* clinics in Santo Domingo," the national capital. "I *ran* their asses off," he blurted, shifting into overt, almost sadistic laughter, like the Marine he always would be, now in charge of whipping umpire candidates into *"Semper Fi"* shape. A transcendental urge had thrust him back to the Carolina swamplands of Camp Lejeune or Parris Island in the role of a wartime Drill Instructor. *"Alto, por favor, Sargento!"* (*"Please, stop, Gunny!"*), his Dominican charges, many of them military veterans and cops, must have been thinking.

"I felt sorry for these guys – the way they were treated in their own country. They got no respect," Garcia said. "You don't treat these people like dogs," he informed the league president and his close *confidants*, referring somewhat to the fact the impoverished country's umpires were not paid to call games despite local fans being among the worst anywhere. These particular *Blue Hombres*, then, were not just low-income; when calling games, they simply were *no*-income.

Garcia contrasted the shabby daily treatment of umpires by their fellow Dominicans with what he considered the positive, quality aspects of healthy, breath-challenging wind sprints. Their behavior *revealed* character; his method *built* character and instilled pride, the former non-com fervently believed.

After compiling a roster of umpiring crews, Garcia set up a post-clinic banquet to acknowledge accomplishments of the largely poor, Third World officiating hopefuls he had run ragged – for their own good, of course.

"When I came back, they all showed up for the banquet, as I had insisted, in coats and ties; they showed pride," Garcia said, his face turning the rosy color of a boastful, grinning father who had just caught that initial glimpse of his first-born through the hospital nursery viewing window.

But here was the *coup de grace* for Rich Garcia: "The league president walked in and saw all these guys – *his umpires* – all dressed up. There was so much pride and excitement in that room with them acting like professionals."

Worked just the way their *Americano* adviser had planned it. *"Must have been the wind sprints,"* Garcia pondered to himself, sticking out his chest and flashing that "New Papa" grin again.

***

Major league umpires acquire their own personal one- or two-digit numbers affixed to the right sleeve of their button-down or polo-style uniform shirts, lined pullover windbreakers or dressier suit coats worn behind the plate. Most, after inquiring whether this special number, or that one, is available, simply resign themselves to accept whichever number MLB assigns them – individual superstition always considered.

Vic Carapazza, a New York-born Florida transplant of Italian ancestry who debuted in The Bigs in 2010 and became full-time before the 2013 season, proudly wears No. 19 – for a very special reason: It is the same number worn by Rich Garcia, in the American League, since 1980, when major league umpires first were assigned numbers. Carapazza, then, when given the opportunity to grab "19" to begin his second season, jumped to dump his previous No. 85. Why? Carapazza calls every game as No. 19 to honor the father of his wife, Stephanie, the youngest daughter among Rich and Sheryl Lynn Garcia's four children.

Carapazza, like his father-in-law, is a military veteran, having served four years in the Air Force including a tour of duty in Kuwait during the Iraq War, whereas Garcia, of course, boasts of a Marine background. The former and his wife, who have four daughters, were sweethearts at Countryside High School in Clearwater, Fla.

Not long after Carapazza, a muscular 6-footer, was honorably discharged in 2005, he surprised Rich Garcia by inquiring about a professional umpiring career. However, Sheryl and Stephanie, having personally experienced the emotional roller coaster that faces MLB umpires' families from early spring through mid-fall every year, intervened at first, respectively giving their son-in-law and husband an emphatic, "No way!" They implored Rich, "Don't let him do it."

Even Rich quietly tried to relate to the former airman, almost forcing him to understand that, while the pay ultimately was gratifying – *if* an individual was both talented and lucky enough to be one of the small percentage of umpire school alumni who got to the majors – the annual byproducts were challenging.

"My one big regret, despite all the rewarding aspects, was spending too much time in the game," Garcia said, recalling advice he had shared with Carapazza, before the son-in-law started to carve out a similar, well-earned career of his own. "There was not enough time with the family," which has grown to include nine grandchildren, for whom retired "free bird" Garcia *makes* time to be part of their varied activities all over the Tampa Bay Area. He and Sheryl were to celebrate their 40th wedding anniversary in October 2016.

As for non-Latino Vic Carapazza, his 2016 season began on a "small world" crew on which he is the youngest member at age 36, headed by a former longtime partner of Rich Garcia's, Connecticut native John Hirschbeck, 61, Garcia's frequent crewmate in the 1990s. Hirschbeck's younger brother, Mark, had been a major league arbiter until health issues ended his career several years ago, making him and John the big league's first brother umpire combination. The other two members of the well-seasoned, all-veteran Hirschbeck crew, are Bill Welke, 49, whose older brother, Tim, is a current MLB crew chief, and their fellow native Michigander, D.J. Reyburn, 40, who, like John Hirschbeck, now lives in Ohio.

Although also not Latino himself, Reyburn was working a winter league game in the Dominican Republic in January 2010 when he was physically assaulted by Licey manager José Offerman, a former major-leaguer. Reyburn had ejected Offerman's catcher for arguing balls and strikes. Offerman was slapped with a lengthy suspension for the attack.

The primary crew on which Carapazza worked most during the 2015 season was led by another longtime professional in his early 60s, Larry Vanover, and also included a 40-something pair, Ron Kulpa and Brian Knight.

***

Garcia and National League counterpart Frank Pulli took a lot of belated heat publicly many years after they had admittedly exercised poor judgment in placing sports bets – none on baseball games – through a Florida bookmaker who was associated with organized-crime figures, an investigation by Major League Baseball concluded. The probe was ordered in 1989 by Fay Vincent, Commissioner of Baseball at the time, who delegated an internal investigator, John Dowd, a special counsel to Vincent, to handle the affair.

A March 8, 2002, investigative report by the *New York Daily News* disclosed that the two umpires had been sanctioned and given two years' probation. The issue was handled internally by Vincent's office, as there was no proof of criminality; it was simply a matter of two longtime officials in a major sport, who had compiled heretofore spotless records and engendered great respect among their peers, having demonstrated lack of basic wisdom, common sense and, as the contrite umpires themselves had admitted, "poor judgment."

"They really did me a favor," Garcia said of the allegations and probe being wake-up calls. "They were all small bets, $25 or less, and I've never bet on sports events since then."

As far as Garcia was concerned, his role in the acknowledged legal, albeit indiscreet, activity was regrettable in retrospect, but the aftermath proved to be essentially much ado about nothing.

"If it had been something so bad, why was I selected to do the World Series as crew chief the same year?" he asked rhetorically in a February 2016 interview for this book.

"Both umpires were cooperative and candid about their conduct with the commissioner and us," Dowd was quoted as saying in a story in *the New York Times* a day following the article in the rival *Daily News.*

Reaffirmation of the pair's collective worth did not stop there.

Said Dowd as late as 2007, in comments to the same *Daily News:* "We know they told the truth because we knew the story before we asked the questions. We did a very thorough investigation," Dowd says. "The punishment fit the crime."

In the 2007 news report, Vincent also weighed in on the action he had taken 18 years before, his assessment echoing other reflections of integrity regarding Garcia and Pulli, and he reiterated his 1989 rationale. "They were high-quality people, and they were dedicated to baseball. Publicizing the disciplinary actions taken against them would have served no purpose," the former commissioner told the New York newspaper that had broken the original story five years earlier.

Someone important and respected who knew the two accused umpires as well as anybody close to the top echelon felt compelled to join the "Hallelujah Chorus" of fairness that publicly heaped deserved praise on them as the case was aired.

"As I said on several occasions, these individuals made a mistake. There were consequences; they went on to have outstanding careers in umpiring and are a credit to the game and to the profession. They performed admirably over a long period of time … There's absolutely no question about their integrity, commitment to the game or to the profession of umpiring," said Sandy Alderson, who was named 2015 Major League Executive of the Year after the New York Mets, for whom he is general manager, won the NL championship. He was MLB executive vice president when the *Daily News* exposé was published in '02. He has been a front office executive in the majors paralleling most of Garcia's AL career and was instrumental in the retired *Blue Hombre's* hiring as an MLB supervisor a year before the damning newspaper account appeared.

***

Rich Garcia was one of as many as nine former veteran umpires who served as MLB umpire supervisors from 2003-2009. They were men, mostly upper middle-age, yet of greatly divergent personal profiles with a varied look in personalities, ethnic and geographic backgrounds and general approach to the game. Their job, collectively and cooperatively, was to ensure, in those who followed them in every ballpark, consistency in behavior, ethics, correct rules interpretation and just good basic grasp of the national pastime at the highest level.

In late '09, however, some wheels came off what had been a seemingly smooth-running vehicle up until then. Following what the most severe critics deemed to be a season of ongoing, on-field miscues, three supervisors among the total staff – the late Marty Springstead, Jim McKean and a fellow named Rich Garcia – were summarily fired, implicated as allegedly the ones most responsible for blown calls by their underlings. (McKean, a Montreal native and former Canadian Football League player who originally aspired to be a National Hockey League referee, had been the third-base umpire for Len Barker's 1981 perfecto.)

Offering his opinion strictly confined to the firing of Garcia, his old buddy and one-time on-field partner, former Crew Chief Bill Haller, declared in a February 2016 interview for this book: "He was innovative, and experimented with ideas. He never should have been let go."

Although Commissioner Bud Selig, who also had hired all three, officially wielded the "axe," the actual executioner was an Ivy League-educated lawyer named Jimmie Lee Solomon who served as Executive Vice President for Baseball Operations from 2005-2010.

Garcia, a Latino from South Florida, and Solomon, an African-American from a rural area outside Houston, Texas, had harbored a long-running feud, fueled by a conflict of two strong-willed personalities. Although self-admittedly never a person himself to judge another by race, the former felt nevertheless there was a racial component to his dismissal, which he believes contributed greatly to his being labeled as one of three scapegoats – the other two dismissed were white. Hence, to equate Garcia to Shakespeare's Othello and Solomon to Othello's antagonist, Iago, would not be far from the truth, especially considering their shared animosities – whatever they may have been – heating up from simmer to boil between 2005, when Solomon was appointed, until Garcia's firing in 2009. Solomon replaced Alderson, who left to take his Mets' executive post.

Again, ever-present irony being what it is, in early June 2012, Solomon either resigned or was fired as Executive VP of Baseball Development, a lesser position to which he was demoted in 2010, purportedly as retrospective "punishment" for the same umpire performance glitches for which Garcia and the two other supervisors had been dismissed the year before. Most news reports of Solomon's departure after 21 years as an MLB executive referred to it as a firing, yet the Commissioner's Office termed it a resignation. Any other specifics to this day remain a carefully guarded secret – keeping in step with all the mysterious occurrences at the top levels of baseball and other major sports.

Garcia, the longest-serving major league umpire of Latino descent, has purposely kept largely mum about his unceremonious exit as a supervisor, preferring not to jeopardize the respected status son-in-law Vic Carapazza has earned, "all on his own," Garcia emphasized to override unfair whispers of imagined "nepotism."

As of March 2016, Solomon touted himself on his personal web site as a business manager for professional athletes, motivational speaker and expert analyst.

***

In between 30 total years as an umpire and seven years supervising them, Garcia served from 2000-2002 as a consultant to the commissioner – the same Bud Selig who would both throw him a life raft, then let him later drown within the span of less than a decade. Selig's tenure of 23 years – from 1992 until he retired and was replaced by MLB Chief Operating Officer Rob Manfred in 2015 – was second only to inaugural Commissioner Kenesaw Mountain "Judge" Landis, who had the top job from 1920-1945.

As for selflessly helping out others, Garcia continued to do that, even after his first Latino crew mate, Armando Rodriguez, had come and gone. For instance, at AL predecessor (1960-69) Bill Kinnamon's Umpire School in Florida, later sold to Garcia's colleague, Joe Brinkman, one acolyte – the youngest member of the 1978 class – was treated with discipline, but also kindness and patience.

"Rich was a good instructor. I learned a lot from him in one month that January. I always enjoyed watching him on televised games whenever possible. That earthquake World Series was kind of scary, though," Jerry Sonnenberg recalled, echoing his one-time teacher's uncharacteristic fear about the natural disaster. Sonnenberg, then 19, was a strapping farm boy from rural Northeast Colorado who went on to become a college umpire and more recently has been a state senator who chairs the Agriculture Committee when not running the family farm outside Sterling, Colo.

***

An independent, non-profit website, which relies heavily on donated information from MLB teams and numerous other sources sharing an unrequited love for baseball, maintains perhaps the most accurate database clearinghouse on the planet for compilation of individual umpire statistics. Working hand-in-hand with the Society for American Baseball Research (SABR) at Arizona State University, Retrosheet.org, founded in 1989 by Dr. David Smith, a University of Delaware biology professor, has compiled a statistical abstract of all major league umpires, present and past, including Rich Garcia. (The Smith-founded organization, similar to projects such as *The Baseball Cube*, works closely with SABR to ensure the most-minute historical accuracy of researching and cataloguing *every pitch* thrown in the major leagues, dating back to 1901.)

According to Retrosheet, Garcia completed a total of 3,398 major league games, among which were 11 games in three AL Division Series, 25 games in five AL Championship Series, 19 games in four World Series, and two All-Star Games. All told, he has umpired the largest amount of his games at third base (871), followed closely by 862 behind the plate, 838 at first base, and 827 at second base. Those numbers do not include postseason breakdowns for assignments down the foul lines in six-man umpire crews.

***

Rich Garcia has regarded any human indiscretions that temporarily beset him during 25 years working AL ballparks basically as minor "hail damage," or small dents in an otherwise-shiny, luxury car of a career. Therefore, while he feels he has contributed positively his entire adult life to baseball enough to dream about possible induction, while still alive to savor it, into the Umpire Wing of the National Baseball Hall of Fame and Museum at Cooperstown, N.Y. (friend and ex-colleague Bill Haller firmly believes "he should be … someday"), he loses no sleep worrying about the "what-if" factor.

Nonetheless, if Garcia never achieves Hall status before he dies, it will not be any harder to swallow than, say, the foul-tasting castor oil his Cuban grandmother gave him for upset stomachs when he was that snot-nosed runt growing up in Key West after World War II.

3
ANGEL HERNÁNDEZ
WINDING UP ON RIGHT SIDE OF WATER

When Angel Hernández takes a moment to reflect on life as it has been, and compares it to an existence that could have been, it makes him smile and realize what a lucky guy he is.

The Major League Baseball umpire – one of more than a dozen *Blue Hombres*, Latinos who have called balls and strikes in the big leagues – is second in tenure in that group only to since-retired fellow Florida resident Rich Garcia, who officiated on American League fields for 25 years in the final quarter of the 20th century. Hernández broke in as a National League "call-up" substitute on May 23, 1991, in a Los Angeles Dodgers' drop-in on the old Houston Astrodome, home of Space City's Astros, then became full-time in the same league in 1993.

In numerology, the year 2016 carried special meaning for Hernández, born in Cuba, but who migrated with his family north across the big water to the Miami, Fla., area when he was a small child. The move occurred not long after his native country saw a sea change in ruling government systems, shifting from Gen. Fulgencio Batista's fascist dictatorship to the equally "strong arm" of Communist revolutionary Fidel Castro, in an armed takeover in 1959, helping hasten the Hernández family's flight north. In that magical 2016, however, the Havana-born but Hialeah-bred umpire finally was to see his age catch up with his uniform number; he was to turn 55 on Aug. 26 of that year, achieving the exact digits as the No. 55 affixed to the sleeve, below the right shoulder, on all his specially designed plate coats, pullover windbreakers and various long- and short-sleeve shirts – each in varying shades of blue. Hernández really wanted "5." It was the number he had

59

worn as an exclusively NL employee, but that already was owned by Dale Scott when all umpires were consolidated as MLBers in 2000, so he settled on his current number, which he never has surrendered. After all, he must have reasoned, a pair of fives, while not exactly a royal flush or full house, still is a semi-decent poker hand.

Most of those closest to him will tell you Angel Hernández is a pleasant, charming, even sometimes shy, gentleman, by most measures, yet on the field of play, he often has been a lightning rod for controversy. This confounds townsfolk in Hialeah, a Miami suburb where he graduated from high school in 1981 and continued to reside with his wife and two daughters until moving, in the mid-'90s, farther up the Gold Coast to a new home in another city, this one a tad more inland from the Atlantic Ocean. It also is noticed by those who have worked closest with him for more than two decades on America's big league baseball diamonds – gracious gentlemen like the venerable Gerry Davis.

"The perception of Angel is distorted a bit," insisted Davis, who has been an MLB crew chief since the day in 2000 the umpires in the two leagues were united into a single force. Before that, Davis, second in tenure only to "Country" Joe West, was an NL arbiter for 22 seasons. "Angel has a heart of gold," added Davis, in an April 2016 interview for this book, the first of multiple Q-and-A sessions with the author between games that month and in May, as another new season began to unfold. Before becoming a crew chief himself, Hernández worked often on crews under Davis's aegis, both in regular-season and postseason settings.

Hernández was a fixture of the community in Hialeah, earning a Key to the City, and numerous awards for youth activities and other civic and charitable causes – things that became off-field habits in his new hometown as well. In Hialeah, his father was founder and longtime director of a youth baseball league, where young Angel, then 14, took his first bite of the umpiring apple, having seen it bloom into an occupational orchard since then. Binks Forest Golf Club, not far from his newer residence in Palm Beach County, honored him for time and financial contributions there by presenting the 6-foot-2, 198-pound outdoors enthusiast with the School Helping Hand Award for his annual charity golf tournament to benefit disabled children.

Consequential to all the well-deserved adulation outside the walls of America's biggest baseball stadiums, Hernández knows this sort of freedom of movement and ability to earn a steady, six-figure annual income would have been a mere pipe dream, if he and his family were instead in Castro's Cuba.

The enigma in all this is: How can such a solid, charitable citizen, well-respected in his community, be so reviled by some managers and players in his chosen profession?

***

Umpires are regarded as equivalent to Cinderella's ugly step-sisters in certain segments of MLB's internal population. There are players, coaches, managers, general managers, team owners and, yes, even hot dog and beer vendors, who never will have pleasant thoughts about the Men in Blue in general. Those critics would rather prefer that umpires focus on being fair (which most are); maintain consistency on calling balls and strikes (which most do, as statistically borne out, both by official and competent non-official sources); and use tact and diplomacy (which most do), even though the arbiters' human side sometimes causes them to react, tit-for-tat, to unwarranted misbehavior by team members from either competing squad.

Gerry Davis insisted that, whether one is taller than 6 feet, as he is, or much shorter, like a few of his competent contemporaries, an umpire must be authoritative and consistent, for certain. However, he added, "Being correct is the *main* thing."

Having officiated games – more than 3,000 of them, according to the unofficial, Canada-based statistical abstract, *The Baseball Cube* – in The Show for nearly 25 full seasons, Angel Hernández is bound to have his critics, and he does. However, when someone survives the barbs and parries *that* long, he also must have his proponents, and he does – Davis a prime example. After all, Hernández is just outside the Top 10, *all time*, in number of postseason games worked, close to the century mark. All-time leader in that regard, with 134 postseason assignments, is Davis himself, eight years Hernández's elder, and with a nine-year MLB seniority edge.

***

Another longtime Hernández friend – and fan – is fiftyish Colorado resident Ken Franek. The latter was a minor league umpire, edging his way up through various rookie and Class A and AA leagues, from the mid-'80s through 1990, when he resigned from the Double-A Carolina League. Back permanently in Colorado, he called games in the Triple-A Pacific Coast League from 1991-95 as a substitute umpire for regulars who were injured or called up to the major leagues.

"I'd work approximately 20 to 30 games a year – all in Colorado Springs," Franek said. "I also worked a few big league exhibition games, when the parent club would play the Triple-A team, in the mid-'90's, such as (Colorado) Rockies vs. (Colorado Springs) Sky Sox, (San Francisco) Giants vs. (Phoenix) Firebirds."

He first met Hernández, whom he described as "a really, really good guy," in 1989 spring training in Florida, at the annual umpire meeting hosted by the Major League Baseball Umpire Development Program. The budding young umpires forged a lifelong friendship in the Sunshine State that continued to shine whenever the Floridian came to Denver with his umpiring crew – whether to share dinner or just banter.

"We all had each other's backs," Franek added, alluding to the cocoon-like comfort zone which somehow was naturally woven into professional umpires' skins – from the day any of them stepped into their inaugural minor league assignment – and forever bound them together as one.

"He deserves to be there" in The Bigs, Franek said of Hernández when interviewed specifically on the topic of *Blue Hombres* in June 2016. That also was a month when Hernández was at sold-out Coors Field to work a two-game, interleague series between the Yankees and Rockies on a Ted Barrett-led crew that also included American-born *Blue Hombre* call-up Gabe Morales and another call-up, Stu Scheurwater, then MLB's lone Canadian umpire since Jim McKean from 1973-2001. (In the worst season for umpire injuries since 2008, call-ups were moving from crew to crew in the first two months of the 2016 campaign more rapidly than a 100-mile-an-hour fastball, so Scheurwater, from Regina, Saskatchewan, transferred to another foursome for the next series, replaced by one of Franek's fellow Colorado natives, Chris Guccione.)

***

Jorge Bauzá, a tireless worker who constantly is on the lookout for new talent to supplement the current complement of MLB umpires with his futuristic outlook, was a contemporary of Hernández's when both were aspiring, young minor league umpires based out of the Miami area in the early '90s. As a result, Bauzá, Field Evaluator/Instructor, MiLB Umpire Development, and Lead Rules Instructor at the MiLB Umpire Training Academy, developed respect for his colleague that has only grown in intervening years.

"I think that Angel is an outstanding umpire," Bauzá said. "He knows the rules, and that they have to be enforced. He's not afraid to enforce the rules," which makes Hernández not always the most popular guy in blue. "Angel is very consistent," the MiLB official added, countering the MLB umpire's critics.

Ken Franek concurred. "Angel is a black-and-white guy" regarding rules interpretations, he said. "There is no gray area."

***

Hailing from a country that has had one kind of dictatorship or another throughout his lifetime so far, Hernández has a special appreciation for "have-not" kids, whether they are economically, physically or mentally disadvantaged.

"I remember being a child and sleeping with my uniform, my trophies, my gloves," the longtime South Floridian told *Palm Beach Post* sports reporter/columnist Tom D'Angelo in a January 2012 interview in conjunction with the second year of the umpire's annual charity tournament at Binks Forest. The initial event a year earlier at Madison Green in Royal Palm Beach, was played to benefit the West Pembroke Pines Miracle League and retired umpires. The 2012 version at Binks Forest solely benefited the Miracle League, which includes youthful physically and mentally disabled players. "What this does for a child that has these disabilities, we can't even imagine. Being there and seeing it, there is no feeling that comes close to it," Hernández related further to the Florida scribe.

The offseason event he sponsors provides the MLB operative a golden opportunity to invite an assortment of present and former umpiring colleagues – among them West, Ed Rapuano, Jerry Layne, Bruce Froemming, Jerry Crawford and Steve Rippley – to mix with such present or ex-players and managers as Larry Walker, Jeff Conine, Bucky Dent, Andres Galarraga, Jim Kaat, Orlando Hernández (no relation to Angel), Tommy Hutton, Joe Smith, Eric Hosmer and Mike Brantley, according to D'Angelo's 2012 column. The charitable atmosphere engenders a brotherly warmth not normally seen openly manifesting itself on baseball diamonds.

"I raised my kids, telling them to stop and say hello to children that are disabled," Hernández also told Tom D'Angelo, underscoring the attitude that trickles down even to non-disabled children, like those of Angel Hernández and his wife, Mireya.

***

The evening Angel Hernández broke in to The Bigs – Thursday, May 23, 1991 – likely carried with it a decent bout of nerves. After all, this was a genuine one-night stand for a kid from Cuba, via Hialeah, Fla.; he would work the game between the Los Angeles Dodgers and Astros in the Houston Astrodome, get a good night's sleep following this momentous occasion, then catch the first flight headed east the next morning to resume his regular, Class AAA International League schedule.

(The IL, completely in the Eastern Time Zone and five states – from Toledo and Columbus, Ohio, on the west; to Rochester and Syracuse, N.Y., the northern outposts; Richmond and Tidewater {Norfolk-Virginia Beach}, way down south in Virginia; and Scranton-Wilkes Barre, Pa., and Pawtucket, R.I., the easternmost clubs – remains the top minor haunt in the East. The league had as colorful a collection of nicknames as existed in baseball at the time: Mud Hens, Clippers, Tides, Chiefs and PawSox. The other remaining Triple-A entity, the Pacific Coast League, absorbed five teams from a disbanded third AAA league, the Midwest-based American Association, in

1997. For a brief period – 1988-91 – before that last league's ultimate demise, it had banded together with the IL to create an interleague partnership called the Triple-A Alliance.)

What alleviated any nervousness somewhat for the 30-year-old tyro from Hialeah were three primary factors. First, the contest was played in the totally enclosed, domed stadium, with a controlled temperature of 70 degrees to save everyone from Houston's oppressive humidity outside the venue. Second, instead of being assigned the "glamour spot" behind home plate, Hernández took his position at the less-sexy third base, replacing Eric Gregg for just the single game. Calling balls and strikes was Crew Chief Dana De Muth, while respectively at first and second bases were two veterans of varying career lengths, Charlie Reliford, who retired in 2009 and became an umpire supervisor, and Mike Winters; Winters still was active and a crew chief in 2016 of what accurately can be dubbed the "M-Squad," with the first names of all its members beginning with the letter M – also including Mark Wegner, Marty Foster and Mike Muchlinski. In third place on the importance ladder that date was the crowd – fewer than 9,000 in the cavernous, so-called "Eighth Wonder of the World" – with front-row seats set back more than most major league ballparks.

(Reliford, by the way, has his name etched permanently in baseball history as crew chief for the first-ever big league game to use the then-new instant review {aka replay} system on a borderline home run call in a Sept. 3, 2008, New York Yankees/Tampa Bay Rays game at tricky, domed Tropicana Field in St. Petersburg, Fla. The Yankees' Alex Rodriguez had hit a ball near the left field foul pole that was ruled a home run by third-base umpire Brian Runge, with his three colleagues concurring with the call. However, Rays Manager Joe Maddon – who more recently has assumed the helm of the Chicago Cubs, for whom he still possesses a perplexing mix of Renaissance Man intellectual discernment with a challenging irascibility toward Men in Blue – argued the ball was foul and asked for a review. By rule, though, the decision to do so was solely Reliford's to make as the crew chief. After huddling with the other umpires, Reliford agreed to the replay and, upon a brief review, upheld the initial home run call.)

In his Astrodome debut, Hernández had to turn and hustle out to left field on a small handful of pop flies and lineouts during a 2-0 combined shutout by Dodgers pitchers Tim Belcher, the starter and winner, John Candelaria and Jay Howell. Oddly enough, the Astros' starter and losing pitcher, who pitched a seven-hitter with no extra-base blows, was Xavier Hernández, also not related to Angel.

Angel Hernández came back up as a full-time NL umpire at the beginning of the 1993 season and, with dozens of other colleagues, was named an MLB umpire when the two major leagues consolidated their crews, as the 21st century began.

***

There was quite a contrast in conditions between Angel Hernández's one-game call-up two years earlier in the indoor, controlled-climate atmosphere of the Houston Astrodome and his permanent debut as an NL umpire. The latter instance, on April 9, 1993, occurred on a windy, drizzly Friday night at Pittsburgh's Three Rivers Stadium, with the Pirates hosting the same opponent who Hernández had seen in the Dome, the Los Angeles Dodgers.

Rather than a paltry gathering of 9,000 spectators like in Houston, though, a modest but more respectably sized crowd of 22,000-plus braved the rains at Three Rivers and, instead of third base, the rookie major league umpire took his spot at first base. He was assigned to a quartet that included the well-respected crew chief, the late Harry Wendelstedt, at second base; another seasoned professional, Randy Marsh, at third; and a younger veteran, Ed Rapuano, calling balls and strikes. Wendelstedt died in 2012, and Marsh and Rapuano retired, respectively, in 2009 and 2012 – each moving on as umpire overseers.

The wet, Dodgers-Pirates collision was an active, nine-inning workout for Angel Hernández in his permanent breakout. He handled safe-out calls on 20 ground balls – three the back end of double plays – and performed a heroic deed for a newbie by calling Pittsburgh left-hander Randy Tomlin for a balk in the top of the second inning.

***

In between his debut in the early '90s and being ever closer to the 25-year-service mark as a big league *Blue Hombre* at the end of the 2016 season, Angel Hernández's résumé includes the 2002 and 2005 World Series; 1999 and 2009 All-Star Games; six League Championship Series – divided evenly between the two leagues (2000, 2001, 2003, 2004, 2007, 2010) – and working in eight League Division Series (1997, 1998, 2002, 2005, 2009, 2011, 2012, 2015). He also did Game 7 of the 2008 ALCS as an injury fill-in for since-retired Derryl Cousins.

***

As a new season dawned on Sunday, April 3, 2016, Hernández found himself in a surprising situation – not personally but regarding the teams in an interleague game at Angel Stadium of Anaheim. Joe Maddon's invading Cubs of the National League blanked the power-laden Los Angeles Angels of Anaheim, 9-0, behind the three-hit pitching of 2015 Cy Young award winner Jake Arrieta, a bearded right-hander who was 22-6 with a stingy 1.77 earned-run average in that shining season and already had pitched no-hitters in consecutive seasons in 2015 and 2016. On his new, 2016 crew, worked first base, and Crew Chief Ted Barrett was behind the plate, with Ross Perot look-alike Lance Barksdale at second and relative newcomer Will Little covering third. The following evening, Hernández grabbed the plate, his mask covering his trademark, shorter-than-normal-brim plate cap; he sailed through the balls and strikes calls in just 2½ hours – quicker than the MLB average – seeing only 243 pitches in a 6-1 Cubs' win.

***

(Author's Note: Angel Hernández was invited to be interviewed for this book, but politely declined. He cited his current active role as an MLB umpire as the main reason. Comments and quotes in this chapter not otherwise original material gathered in exclusive interviews of others by the author, or otherwise directly attributed within the chapter, are cited and listed in Source Notes at the back of this book.)

4
LAZ DÍAZ
PRESENTING A 'DIFFERENT' ASPECT

Major League Baseball (MLB) umpires are like their counterparts in the Nationals of other big-time sports: the National Basketball Association, the National Football League and the National Hockey League – they do not relish being attention-craving "hot dogs." There are, though, those individuals among their collective ranks who have personalities that automatically make them the "spicy mustard" spread on the "frankfurter" to perk-up the overly priced tube-steak meal so common at the nation's ballparks.

Whether one or another MLB umpire intends to be the center of attention has been debated since 1869, when – the much-disputed origins of the National Pastime not totally agreed upon – Abner Doubleday, or someone, concocted a new sport which used a horsehide ball and a stick to strike at it. However, there *are* somewhat off-kilter personalities who frequently emerge, and they *have* to hog the spotlight because a certain dose of unorthodox behavior is simply part of their being.

This explanation may seem counter to what all these leagues' commissioners, presidents, team owners, and even players, expect of the mostly competent, proven professional types who officiate their sports. That boiler-plate view of umpires, referees, linesmen, side judges, back judges and the like who are expected to be cookie-mold automatons is noble, but probably obsolete, in our "look-at-me-and-my-selfie" society.

Therefore, perhaps we must, as a general fandom, forgive, forget and move forward in instances of "spontaneous combustion" by an ump or ref who, without warning, suddenly – and maybe surprisingly – revs his engine in a here-and-gone display that lasts mere seconds like a Funny Car roaring down a drag strip.

There is necessarily no specific manner in which this happens, and no particular explanation as to "why," except for the foibles of human nature – purely and simply. Even veteran baseball umpires who earn professional plaudits from their peers and superiors are susceptible to such quirks.

Enter from Stage Right through a figurative proscenium arch that more resembles a dugout tunnel: Lazaro Antonio Díaz, Sr. Known to almost everyone simply as Laz, he is a walking, talking contradiction. A big league umpire since 1995, becoming what is referred to as an "up-and-down" guy, he first worked exclusively in the American League, then was transformed into an MLB ball-and-strike caller at the turn of the new millennium, with all top-level baseball umpires merged into one entity. Except for 1997, between 1995-1998, Díaz worked a total of 41 AL games, as an up-and-down operative shuttling often from the Triple-A International League to the Junior Circuit and vice-versa. The Orlando resident was hired as an essentially full-time AL arbiter in 1999, when he called 84 games.

But here's the deal: Laz Díaz internally almost always receives high marks and praise from umpire supervisors and crew peers – those who possess the expertise to evaluate his performance most accurately. Yet, to the public – and sportswriters, bloggers, some announcers and other critical observers – he is perceived as inconsistent, sometimes ornery and distant.

"He has a great baseball background," fellow Miami resident and former minor league umpire Jorge Bauzá said of Díaz. Bauzá's job, among several baseball-related functions he juggles on a daily basis, is to recruit and develop new professional umpires – domestically and from other countries. Díaz's own résumé includes a season of playing Class A professional baseball before changing direction to enroll in umpire school – a move he said he never will regret.

"Laz is an outstanding umpire. He knows the game, and is always willing to help Latin (American) umpires who come into the system," added Bauzá, who also is responsible specifically for professional baseball's focus on finding potential talent in the Caribbean, Mexico, and South and Central America.

However, that teaching touch by Díaz extends to non-Latino up-and-comers as well – for instance, 26-year-old MLB rookie Nic Lentz, youngest big league umpire in 2016.

"Common sense is common sense," Díaz told this author in an interview exclusively for this book, relaxing in a cool hotel lobby on a 90-degree-plus, late June day before working that night at Denver's Coors Field. He had been scheduled to meet an old, familiar face – Toronto's Canadian-born catcher, Russell Martin – but agreed with Crew Chief Jeff Nelson to give young call-up umpire Lentz an added opportunity to crouch behind Martin after a severe turn in the weather that evening. The start of that Colorado Rockies' game against the Blue Jays was delayed for nearly three hours by a wicked thunderstorm that dumped several inches of rain and marble-size hail on the tarpaulin-covered playing surface. Díaz, a lifelong Floridian who rarely sees hail or even snow, was spotted during the long delay tossing hail stones into the air like a merry juggler. With Lentz on the plate, Díaz grabbed third base, where he could carefully observe the newer guy, leaving Nelson at second, and Denver area native Cory Blaser at first. Lentz made his big league debut on April 20, 2016, stationed at first in a Washington Nationals-at-Miami Marlins game on a crew with umpire school honcho Hunter Wendelstedt, Scott Barry and Tripp Gibson.

The Nelson crew then traveled intact to New York's Citi Field, where the next series – Mets versus best-record-in-baseball Chicago Cubs – included a nationally viewed Fox network Saturday telecast that had Díaz calling balls and strikes.

With Laz Díaz, once a game begins, there is no juggling of the rulebook for this ardent arbiter. Business is business and, as he firmly put it, "Rules are rules. You can't bend the rules," the otherwise affable Díaz added, demonstrating the stern rigidity of the typical, veteran major league umpire.

Rich Garcia, the living "dean" of the *Blue Hombres* and U.S. Marine veteran who called AL games for a quarter-century, still was in the league for Díaz's first five seasons – some with the Miami native as a member of a Garcia-headed crew. Then, for a period totaling nearly a decade in the early 2000s, Garcia was able to monitor MLB umpires – including his fellow

Sunshine State resident – first as a consultant to Commissioner Bud Selig, followed by a seven-year stint as one of nine umpire supervisors.

Garcia, who is capable of being hyper-critical as warranted, nonetheless heaped praise on Díaz when asked to assess his one-time colleague. Replying to questions from the author of this book during an exclusive interview in March 2016, Rich Garcia said: "Laz worked with me quite a lot, plus I've watched him develop over the years. He's a good umpire who has developed into a very good umpire.

"He is very colorful," Garcia added regarding the 5-foot-11, 200-pound current umpire, who opened the 2016 season on a crew helmed by Mike Everitt that also included Tim Timmons and Paul Emmel. Their first series together as a crew in the new campaign was a four-game set from April 3-6 at St. Petersburg's Tropicana Field in which the defending AL champion Blue Jays defeated Tampa Bay's Rays, 5-3, in the first two contests – not once, but twice, by the identical score. The Rays captured Game Three in a 3-2 squeaker. Díaz, who had begun the series at third base, then rotated around, respectively, to cover the other pair of "bags," was behind the plate for the final verdict – a second consecutive Rays' win by a score of (you guessed right) 5-3.

(Later in 2016, as the season moved through its worst injury year for the Men in Blue since 2008, Emmel was added to the casualty list – one pitch away from being able to complete a June 23 night game between the Oakland Athletics and the host Los Angeles Angels of Anaheim. With Oakland leading, 5-4, and two outs in the top of the ninth inning, the Athletics' closer, Sean Doolittle, the southpaw with the thick, red beard, served up a first pitch to Angels pinch-hitter Jefry Marté, a product of Puerto Rico, who swung and missed. However, in the process, Marté lost control of his bat, which flew right over crouching Oakland catcher Stephen Vogt and directly to Emmel's head, as he was squatting in his preferred "scissors" stance, with his head deep in the "slot," just over Vogt's left shoulder. The blow, in which the bat's barrel struck the plate umpire's face mask, did not knock Emmel unconscious, but caused a gushing gash along his left hairline that was treated with 11 stitches. Emmel, on this fateful night, crew chief of a different group of umpires than that with which he had begun the season nearly three months earlier, was replaced by third base partner Quinn Wolcott, with Emmel's fellow Colorado resident Mike Di Muro and Mark Carlson remaining on the bases until the final out – a pop-up by Marté on the next pitch to Dominican Republic native second baseman Arismendy Alcántara – preserved a one-run Oakland victory.)

Díaz, who had managed to remain virtually injury-free through the 2016 All-Star break, attributed the general injury increase among his colleagues to more pitchers throwing harder, and a resulting frequency of harder-hit baseballs.

To describe Díaz, who served 12 years in the Marine Reserves and still actively supports veterans' causes, the way Garcia did would be the understatement of the year. Laz Díaz, you see, does not consciously try to call attention to himself; it is just that he naturally reacts to varied situations with what Garcia describes as "presenting a different aspect."

Many times, the retired official confided, "he handles situations differently than the average umpire. He'd rather talk to you and stem a crisis, instead of going after you ... and I say that in a good way ... in today's world," said Garcia, who was born in Key West, Fla., but has lived most of his adult life up the Gulf Coast in the Tampa Bay Area.

As a consequence of Díaz's manner, since his first big league game in 1995, he has among the lowest rates of ejecting players, managers and coaches of all his peers, and also a very stingy strike zone. Like Garcia, he is of Cuban ancestry, was born and raised in an immigrant family in South Florida and is capable of an infrequent "volcanic eruption," yet, also like his former *compadre*, Díaz exemplifies patience, strict adherence to the rules of the game and just a general respect for its history and traditions.

Hence, such rigidness caused him perhaps the most grief of his career in an incident involving then-New York Yankees' catcher Martin in a May 2012 game in California against the host Los Angeles Angels of Anaheim. (The Bard-worthy drama of the Díaz-Martin saga – replete with full moons and other ghostly gambits rarely evident unless a baseball diamond is in some remote Iowa cornfield – is discussed more in-depth later in this chapter.)

The Angels have been owned since 2003 by self-made billionaire businessman Arturo "Arte" Moreno, the first Mexican-American owner of a major American sports franchise. Moreno, oldest of 11 children and a U.S. Army Vietnam veteran, was simultaneously praised by the average fan for lowering ticket and beer prices at his team's playing venue, but criticized by Anaheim city officials and Angels diehards in 2003 and 2005, respectively, for changing the stadium's and team's names.

Created as a major league expansion franchise in 1962 and simply dubbed the Los Angeles Angels (a bilingual redundancy), the organization played its initial two seasons as a "tenant" in Dodger Stadium, and became the California Angels upon moving southeast 30 miles to Orange County four years later. The team was called the Anaheim Angels from 1978 until Moreno bought the franchise, changing the name again.

The stadium, still with a fairly modern look despite being baseball's fifth-oldest playing site, was originally called Anaheim Stadium before morphing into Edison International Field of Anaheim in 1997, amid the naming-rights wave, which has allowed major businesses to pay team owners well into eight figures to have their company's moniker adorn the arena's name. It sits less than three miles east of Disneyland – quite appropriate in that the Walt Disney Co. was the club's owner which sold the franchise to Moreno for $180 million. (The stadium's previous Edison name was derived from the millions in naming-rights dollars paid by the local electric utility, Southern California Edison.)

Regardless of its several formal names, most baseball followers still refer to it simply as "The Big A," an accurate description that mirrors the giant, red steel tower outside the park's main entrance replicating the team logo, high-hung halo and all.

***

Join us now back at The Big A on May 30, 2012, as we return to center-stage from a brief intermission to Act II of the neo-Shakespeare presentation of *Laz vs. Russell*:

On a typically balmy, Southern California evening, Laz Díaz is cruising along behind the plate in an AL interdivisional, bicoastal contest matching two teams on the borderline between early season success and struggle – the 27-23 Yankees and the 26-26 Angels. The visiting New Yorkers enter the game at Angel Stadium in third place in the AL East, but just 1½ games behind division pacesetter Baltimore; the Halos, despite the .500 record, sit in second place in their division, trailing the AL West-leading Texas Rangers by 5½.

Temperatures hover in the upper 60s, and a nice breeze averaging 8 miles per hour blows across the "dish," straight toward center field. Ergo, Díaz is comfortable in having chosen his navy blue, long-sleeve, button-down, cotton-woven shirt – his No. 63 emblazoned in white on the upper right sleeve – which not only is durable but matches the color of the giant, knit ball bag hooked to his wide, black belt and slipped easily over his inside chest protector. That number, as is also the case with at least five other MLB contemporaries, signifies Díaz's birth year of 1963. (A really good "chest" protector, like those used in The Bigs and discussed in the Introduction, also covers both shoulders and upper-arm areas, without unfashionably "peeking" out as if it did not belong there.)

Whatever comfort the Miami-born-and-bred plate umpire – who in recent years has lived in Orlando – had felt at the game's outset slowly starts disappearing, as the minutes and innings tick off without notice in the ultimate clock-less sport.

Speaking of "ticked off," all game long, Díaz and the Yankees' experienced and well-traveled catcher, Montreal-born Martin, have engaged in a sort of contest of wits, it seems – Martin unhappy with the umpire's characteristically tight strike zone, and fearing ejection if he offers one too many "suggestions." Perhaps Martin, who admits to never having had any past problems with Díaz, though, either is unaware of, or chooses to ignore that, *this* specific umpire has that lower-than-normal ejection rate and, thus, is not prone to "toss" anyone except the most-egregious naysayer. In other words, Laz Díaz, despite some misperceptions to the contrary, based on his effusive personality, is an athletic official who possesses great patience – until, and if, the wrong "button" ultimately is pushed.

Apparently, this late-spring night in Anaheim signals Russell Martin to lean too hard on the wrong buzzer, as if he were playing a television game show at a Southern California studio rather than a big league baseball contest not far from Hollywood and, of course, ever so much closer to the Magic Kingdom.

In a detailed account the next day in one of New York's collection of well-opinionated, acerbic daily newspapers, the outspoken catcher insists: "Laz, actually, had hurt my feelings. The umpire wouldn't let me throw the ball back to the pitcher. That's something that's never happened to me before." *The catcher in the "wry" doth protest too much*, the needle on the stage-left irony meter indicates, as it jiggles back and forth spastically.

Martin continues to vent in the day-after game account: "He said that it was a privilege for me to earn, to throw the ball back ... because we kind of got into it on balls and strikes or whatever. ... That was strange. I was kind of mystified."

Again, this demonstrates a short, and selective, memory by Russell Martin, whose feelings probably *are* hurt, because he is used to doing the throw-backs to the mound himself.

What the Bronx-based backstop forgets is the professional protocol practiced by Díaz, especially late in the game, when a foul ball goes straight to Martin's neck, automatically rendering the home plate umpire to call "time." Seeing what had just happened to the catcher, Díaz, out of courtesy and to give Martin extra recovery time, walks slowly to the mound to hand the ball to New York reliever Rafael Soriano, and eases back around to resume his "squat," inquiring about the player's well-being as he passes alongside him.

Soriano finishes off the Angels in the top of the ninth to earn a save and preserve a 6-5 victory. Yet, even with that, Martin is not satisfied, according to the next day's story.

"We really didn't talk that much, until I got hit in the neck. Then he had to kind of go out to the mound. I know he didn't want to, but he did," the Yankee keeps complaining.

As for Díaz, a double minority who is a black of Cuban descent, it is likely he had witnessed his share of the ancient spiritual practices of *Santeria* and

76

voodoo growing up among relatives in and around Miami's Little Havana and officiating winter league games all over the Caribbean. Therefore, even though the ever-present thick smog common to Southern California likely obscures the moon on this eerie evening, he maybe is pondering vampires, werewolves and other creatures when Díaz is rumored to comment, after the game, to one of his umpire partners, upon hearing Martin's free-wheeling comments: "There must have been a full moon." Indeed – just as that lunar orb is rising over Sleeping Beauty's Castle a mere couple miles away in the Magic Kingdom.

***

Years before – on April 15, 2003 – Tax Day proved to be particularly taxing, physically rather than fiscally, for first base umpire Laz Díaz, who, like all professional sports game-callers, was getting used to absorbing psychological beatings administered by screaming fans in big league ball yards everywhere.

"Kill the ump!" "Three blind mice!" "Here, take my glasses; you need them more than me!" And frequent insertion of four-letter words and personal epithets (*"Why, you, blankety-blank!"*) made these mostly one-way "discussions" (more accurately, diatribes) notably toxic – and potentially threatening.

Rarely, however, would anyone with even half a wit of sense ever consider venturing beyond the vicious, yet merely verbal, attacks by violating the sanctity of the National Pastime and actually leaping out of the stands to bodily assault an umpire or player.

This was a different kind of day, though, at the Windy City's South Side baseball emporium, U.S. Cellular Field, the "lipstick-on-a-pig" designation slapped on ancient Comiskey Park as the remodeled home of the Chicago White Sox. Yet, regardless of the rarity of the moment, what was about to occur would mark the repeat of a similar, ugly incident seven months earlier, which had happened during the 2002 season.

On Sept. 10, 2002, an ill-advised father-son pair, William Ligue, Jr., and William Ligue, III, both highly intoxicated, wielding at least one knife and with bad intent, jumped the low fence down the right-field line, proceeding to attack – without warning or letting up – Kansas City Royals' 54-year-old first-base coach, Tom Gamboa. Gamboa, who moved to relative shelter as KC bullpen coach the following season, had survived the onslaught, and security was increased at "The Cell" (which some Chisox fans and pundits varyingly refer to as Comiskey II, Comiskey, Jr., or Son of Comiskey) and other MLB fields. Despite the seriousness and overt public nature of their crime, and Gamboa's resultant diagnosis of a hearing loss, the Ligues never got their own *cell* – the iron-barred variety – to call home, receiving only probation in Chicago's hard-to-fathom judicial system.

This day in April 2003, then, was about to be one that fit the trite niche where history *does* indeed repeat itself. And the unsuspecting target was a Marine reservist named Laz Díaz, a *Blue Hombre*, or one of roughly a dozen or so Latino men who have worked as major league umpires since the first one – here-one-year-gone-the-next Cuban *émigré* Armando Rodriguez – debuted in 1974.

The fan, later identified as 25-year-old Eric Dybas, entered the playing surface, a somewhat sanctified stretch of sod trodden upon during games only by "authorized personnel," from about the same physical point as did the errant Ligues. Dybas, who was charged with assault and battery and did six months' jail time, obviously chose the wrong victim in the bulky, muscular Floridian.

As he would reportedly do nine years later, Díaz invoked a lunar reference, telling reporters, "We thought nothing was going to happen. I bet there was a full moon out there," waving his arms in an expressive manner generally toward the cosmos.

There had been a premonition of sorts in the umpires' locker room in pre-game preparations, said Díaz, commenting reflectively to the "newsies" following the game: "We talked about it in the locker room; this is the place where Tom Gamboa got attacked." After repeating his full moon mention, Díaz continued: "He just grabbed me by my waist," he said of his assailant, "and that's when I turned around and got him down, and everybody just jumped on him."

The assault had happened a moment following Díaz going out to right field on a fly ball by Chicago's Carlos Lee to end the bottom of the eighth inning, and upon the unsuspecting return to the "rim," where the infield dirt and outfield grass intersect, to await the start of the ninth inning. However, all of a sudden, Dybas approached quickly from the foul line, unaware that the longtime Leatherneck was about to unleash his old defensive can of "whoop-ass," turning the young miscreant's one-man siege into an old-fashioned *Semper Fi* counterattack.

"When I looked over, I saw one of the fans from the stands, and I just got him off me. I just turned around and got him off me. The good hand-to-hand combat they taught me (in the Marine Corps) worked," said Díaz, who was able to finish unscathed, with KC coming from behind to win, 8-5. Ironically, the White Sox starter and loser that day, southpaw Mark Buehrle, would play a role in a career highlight for the attacked umpire six years later during Laz Díaz's continuation of his own personal Shakespeare Festival.

The underlying solidarity that exists – despite an adversarial, yet respectful, cat-and-mouse relationship – among on-field "authorized personnel," coupled with that previously mentioned sanctity, was underscored the day of the crime in postgame comments by Royals' catcher Mike Sweeney.

"As a major league baseball player, you shouldn't have to worry about your health on the baseball field from a fan," Sweeney told assembled reporters, tacitly meaning to include umpires, managers and coaches with players as protected classes against in-game criminal acts. "When they come on the field to do harm, that's scary!" (This issue, amid the increasing threat of terrorism, will be addressed further in Chapter 5.)

The other members of Díaz's umpire crew the day of the Dybas assault were:

- **Dale Scott,** Home Plate, who "came out" prior to the 2015 season as MLB's first openly gay umpire;

- **Jim Reynolds,** Second Base, who was on the crew officiating Philadelphia Phillies ace Roy "Doc" Halladay's perfect game against host Miami in May 2010 and joined Venezuelan-born *Blue Hombre*

Manny Gonzalez with CB Bucknor on crew chief Fieldin "Cubby" Culbreth's foursome at the outset of the 2016 season;

- And **Jim Joyce**, Third Base, an Ohioan with perhaps with the loudest strike call in the majors who admitted afterward he cost Detroit's Armando Gallaraga a perfecto with a blown call at first base versus Cleveland in June 2010.

***

In a Thursday afternoon game on July 23, 2009, Laz Díaz was working third base at the same site, "The Cell," on Chicago's South Side, where he had been physically assaulted by fan Eric Dybas six years earlier. Handling the plate this time was burly Eric Cooper, a guy who, like Doug Eddings, likes to step out from his position and fire fastballs back at pitchers rather than handing the ball gently to a catcher when bringing a new horsehide into play. They were joined by two since-retired umpires, Mike Reilly and Chuck Meriwether, at first and second base, respectively. (It would be interesting indeed to ask someone like Laz Díaz critic Russell Martin if he feels the same "offense" when serial fastball-flingers such as Cooper and Eddings also are ignoring his desire for the toss-back.)

The occasion on an uncharacteristically pleasant, 69-degree day – for Chicago in midsummer, when high temperatures typically soar at least into the muggy 90s – would turn out to be the 18th perfect game in big league history. This time it was the host White Sox's southpaw ace, Mark Buehrle, who mowed down all 27 Tampa Bay batters he faced. The burly Buehrle, whose physique is similar to Eric Cooper's, barely had missed a previous perfecto by issuing only a base-on-balls to the Texas Rangers' Sammy Sosa in a no-hitter two years before.

With no visiting base runners to keep him company at the Hot Corner all day, Díaz's main exercise that afternoon when the Rays were batting consisted of his hustling out to short left field on five fly balls to make a cursory "out" sign. Any other physical activity in the 5-0 Chisox win was provided by the locals.

***

Díaz was at second base on Aug. 7, 2007, at San Francisco's AT&T Park to witness first-hand and up-close Barry Bonds's 756th career home run, breaking Hank Aaron's record, in a match-up of Bond's Giants and the Washington Nationals. His crew mates in that night game were plate man John Hirschbeck, the late Wally Bell at first and Bill Welke at third.

***

In an MLB umpiring career dating back to the mid-'90s, Lazaro Antonio Díaz, Sr., himself a veteran, has given autographed baseballs to, or at least personally acknowledged, fans who obviously also had served in the military. And like current fellow *Blue Hombres* Angel Hernández and Alfonso Marquez, he never turns down an invitation to visit places such as Shriners' hospitals and other locales where there are disabled children. Despite his natural flair for showmanship, Díaz often accomplishes this without much fanfare.

Similar as well to Hernández, also a Floridian of Cuban descent, Díaz approaches real-life situations that require compassion as an example for his own children.

"We have a reputation on the field, and we have a reputation off the field. We're all fun-loving. We all have families back home. We all have kids," Díaz told a Baltimore newspaper during an August 2014 visit to Johns Hopkins Children Center's oncology unit.

The umpiring pair's philanthropy and regular volunteer charity work obviously has not gone unnoticed, especially in the Cuban-related community. Being the two major league umpires who worked with four Cuban national colleagues, in a spring 2016 exhibition contest pitting the victorious Tampa Bay Rays against the Cuban National Team in Havana, landed both Díaz and Hernández in the Cuban Sports Hall of Fame.

"It was a good experience," Díaz told the author of this book. "My family, who I hadn't seen in a long time, drove 4½ hours (from Santa Clara, in eastern Cuba) to get there" for the game, in which Hernández served as umpire crew chief.

Even before the Cuba exhibition, the period encompassing the 2012 through 2014 seasons also had proved momentous – depending on individual interpretation of different events – for Díaz becoming perhaps more known for his fast feet than his *per se* umpiring. In an Aug. 6, 2014, Houston Astros/Philadelphia Phillies game at Citizens Bank Park, he opted, in between innings, to dance the *salsa* with the famed mascot, the Phillie Phanatic. With nearly 30,000 YouTube views generated, it will not permit the umpire to have complete peace and final closure on the incident. He must have expected post-dance reviews to be more "loving" in the City of Brotherly Love.

***

All told, by the end of the 2015 season, Laz Díaz had logged more than 40 postseason games. The most recent was the 2015 AL Championship Series won by the eventual World Series winners, the Kansas City Royals, over the Blue Jays. Overall, he has completed more than 2,100 contests in the regular season – roughly 500 or so at each position – and he worked the 2000 and 2010 All-Star Games.

***

Rich Garcia, one of Díaz's earliest on-field role models and former crew chief who has watched his ex-pupil evolve, as the retired umpire later became an observer from afar in his supervisory role, said he has "seen the development" in Díaz, who was to turn 53 in summer 2016.

"When I suggested something to him, he took it to heart," Garcia said. "As far as being a good student, he was." He further implied that his one-time acolyte "might even become a good supervisor someday."

That assessment is no surprise because of mutual respect that has developed between the U.S.-born descendants of Cuban ancestors.

"Richie is my mentor – an umpire's umpire," Díaz said, echoing the awe often voiced by countless other MLB colleagues, Latino or not, about the well-respected, outgoing guy who has called the most balls and strikes of any *Blue Hombre* ever.

5
ALFONSO MARQUEZ
SUCCESS BEGETS PASSING THE TORCH

"D*ate prisa! Pon la pelota en el bate y pégale a mí, estúpido!*

On a dusty rockpile bearing a vague resemblance to a baseball diamond in the village of La Encarnación, Zacatecas, Mexico, a couple dozen eager boys, ages 7 to 9, have gathered informally and begun a makeshift game. It is early December 1979, just before Christmas, on a 72-degree day – not uncommon in late fall in the largely arid, 6,000-feet-high north-central Mexico plains, wedged between two lofty mountain ranges.

The second baseman, perhaps emulating one of his country's horsehide heroes of the past several decades – possibly a pitcher such as Fernando Valenzuela, Aurelio Lopez, Vicente Romo or Horacio Pina, maybe current sluggers like Jorge Orta and Aurelio Rodriguez, or infielder Bobby Ávila, the Cleveland Indians' league batting champion and 1954 World Series star – is exhorting the opposing batter: "Hurry up! Put the ball on the bat and hit it to me, stupid!"

The fielder is a little guy, all of 4-feet-6, named Alfonso Marquez. It turns out that the other miniature *hombre* – the *niñito* with bat in hand – is Alfonso's best friend, his *compadre*, Antonio, the *tocayo*, or namesake, of his friend Alfonso's father, but the younger Antonio is known more endearingly merely as "Tony." Little Alfonso, who some call by the diminutive, "Poncho," normally is a clear-headed kid, not taken by impetuousness. Yet lately he has shown impatience around his mother, Hermelinda, and slightly older sister, Cecilia. The reason? Late in the previous summer, Antonio Marquez, the head of the family in their house without running water and with "dinner by candlelight" the nightly ritual, left to make a new life in *El Norte*, the United

States – specifically Southern California. Not to abandon his wife and children. No. He would cross the border, without papers, but having paid a *coyote* "group escort" a greatly inflated sum of money he could ill afford; set up stakes and find work in any one of dozens of older suburbs around Los Angeles that had attracted other undocumented workers like himself willing to do tough jobs; and then would somehow figure out a way to have his family reunite with him in California.

"We had an outhouse my dad had made out of a corral," Alfonso Marquez, now having just turned 44, remembered, today being more than able to have his own horses, rather than do his "business" outside among the equines. "We had a pig in there, a cow for milk, and lots of chickens running around.

"In addition to not having running water, we also had no electricity; just a lot of candles" – a typical scenario in rural Mexico even to this day, in some regards.

Papa Antonio, loyal, hard-working guy he was, naturally kept his promise to Hermelinda, Alfonso and Cecilia. Therefore, less than two months after his son played in the "sandlot" ballgame atop the makeshift, rocky diamond, Antonio had earned enough to pay another *coyote* nearly $1,000 U.S. dollars to gather his loved ones, and transport them, via Tijuana and San Ysidro, on a nearly week-long journey of unification.

The Marquezes later would add another daughter, named Hermelinda, after her mother. Alfonso Marquez's parents and two sisters – the younger one now 29 – still live in or around Orange County, while the family's only son, Alfonso, has since relocated with his wife, Staci, to the Phoenix suburb of Gilbert, Ariz., a strategic move that has made much sense in a year-round fashion, as his redemptive and heartwarming personal story continues to unfold.

***

Fast-forward just a little more than 20 years after the improvised kids' ball game in rural Zacatecas state, as the video cam held by now-30-year-old Alfonso Marquez, already known to friends and colleagues as the Americanized "Fonzy," rather than the more traditional "Poncho," pans the same once-rocky spot where the youthful, informal teams had congregated.

The site has been transformed over two decades into a grassy, fenced, genuine baseball field that is part of the sprawling *Actividades Deportivas Campus Zacatecas* (Sports Activities Complex) Southern Campus of Villaneuva, the much larger, surrounding municipality that has since annexed La Encarnación.

Accompanying Alfonso Marquez, now a Major League Baseball umpire, are his two best friends, fellow arbiter Ted Barrett, and Jorge Bauzá, a Puerto Rico-born former professional umpire himself who balances various responsibilities on a daily basis related to minor league umpire evaluation and instruction, and searching for umpiring talent in Caribbean locales. The three *amigos* are part of a contingent that has arrived in Mexico to assess prospective umpiring talent, and also as leaders in a Good Samaritan charitable effort to offer donated new and used serviceable officiating equipment they have collected to Latin American baseball programs.

In addition, the humanitarian pursuit provided the emphasis for Marquez to birth "Fonzy's Kids," a personal non-profit whose activities were detailed in a July 8, 2007, story in *The Orange County Register,* the county-wide daily newspaper whose coverage includes Fullerton, where he and family eventually settled, and where it first occurred to him that there really was something to this thing called umpiring.

"A great friendship developed" with Marquez, said Bauzá, because of common goals, especially those associated with a topic close to both their hearts – creating a wealth of *Blue Hombres*, or Latino-descent umpires from all over the *beisbol*-loving Western Hemisphere, ideally from the tip of Cape Horn to the Arctic Circle and everywhere in between, if possible.

"He's just like a brother to me," Marquez said of Bauzá. He was echoing precisely the sentiment Bauzá always professes when talking about Marquez or any of the other umpires with whose professional lives the Puerto Rico native has become closely involved.

The pair had begun to formulate strategy as informal advisors to the Mexican League, a Class AAA-level confederation not officially affiliated with MLB or MiLB, nonetheless huddling even in the Baseball Commissioner's New York office one offseason.

"Then, 10 years ago, we went to Mexico – the first time an American, the first time a Mexican-American (Marquez), helped to train Mexican umpires," said Bauzá, who also serves in several non-MiLB capacities in conjunction with the Caribbean Confederation and its annual Caribbean World Series.

***

The close alliance between "Fonzy" Marquez, who had grown to 5-11 and 200 pounds, and Ted Barrett, who seemed to be 6-4 and 255 all his life, advanced fairly quickly from professional to personal. They often were assigned to the same four-man umpire crew after MLB unified American and National League umpires in 2000 into a single entity, with umpires able to work in both leagues. Following his full-time umpiring debut in 1993 in the Class A Northwest League, Marquez worked in the minors until 1999, when called up to join the regular NL staff. The following season, he and Barrett, 50, were among those hired to be MLB umpires on the heels of an unsuccessful, union-organized umpire work stoppage in '99. Since he came to the majors nearly 17 years ago, Fonzy Marquez has worn No. 72 on his umpire uniform; it signifies his birth year of 1972.

According to Laz Díaz, a *Blue Hombre* colleague of Marquez and Barrett whose personal story was related in Chapter 4, the genesis for the uniform-number/birth-year tie-in was at the turn of the 21st century, when the three were part of the much larger group of former AL and NL umpires who were consolidated into the single entity.

Demonstrating he would be a tricky poker-playing partner, never betraying a straight face, Díaz told the author of this book during a June 2016 interview in Denver, "When we got hired, there were five of us" who chose such numbers – "Me, Ted, Fonzy, Lance (Barksdale) and Bruce Froemming; all of us picked our birth years. So Bruce chose 6, for 1906." Froemming was by far the senior member of the converts, but actually was born in 1939. Since then, at least one other MLB umpire, Venezuelan Manny Gonzalez (subject of Chapter 6), has adopted the practice.

While calling ball in the minors, Fonzy Marquez "moonlighted" in the offseason at the now-defunct Brinkman-Froemming Umpire School in

Florida. The school was operated by two colorful longtime, since-retired major league umpires, the AL's Joe Brinkman and the NL's Froemming. The two continued to officiate after starting the school, which they operated during the offseason each January. Brinkman originally had bought the school from ex-major league umpire Bill Kinnamon in the 1970s.

Barrett, who was ordained a minister in 2007 and also is co-founder (with MLB umpire Rob Drake) of Calling for Christ, a professional umpire ministry, came into Fonzy Marquez's world at a time when the latter needed help most in his off-field personal life.

Living the nomadic existence of a big league umpire is nothing new to the affable Barrett, who carries an imposing presence into every stadium, but to those who know him best, he is nothing more than, well, a big *Teddy* bear.

With a father whose business and military travels took him and his family literally everywhere, Barrett, born in Washington state, has lived as both a child and adult in such diverse locales as upstate New York, the Midwest and the San Francisco Bay Area. He found time over several offseason periods to earn a bachelor's degree from California State University Hayward (now East Bay), where he played football in the 1980s, then procured a master's in biblical studies from Trinity Seminary and added his PhD in theology with emphasis on pastoral studies from Trinity Theological Seminary. He also competed for a while as an amateur boxer and was a sparring partner for several well-known heavyweight champions, including George Foreman, Evander Holyfield and Mike Tyson.

"I've often asked him when he has time to eat, sleep, preach, umpire baseball, and still spend quality moments with his family. He's quite a remarkable man, and a great role model for kids, regardless of color or social status," Fonzy Marquez said of Barrett, a middle-age "vanilla" white guy with a large, economy-size heart.

***

When Marquez was sidelined for the 2009 season with almost-crippling back problems, he had to do a lot of retrospective soul-searching about drinking, marital infidelity and other assorted behavior that already was beginning to subside – and disappear completely – as he matured and eventually married his second wife, Staci.

The literal result? He turned to Jesus, guided by Barrett and an unconventional, itinerant preacher from Oklahoma named Dean Esskew. The traveling clergyman is known simply as Pastor Dean, a self-avowed non-sports fan who professes to hate baseball. Nevertheless, he shows up everywhere, preaching the Gospel to – and baptizing – umpires, athletes and other sports figures, claiming it is returning a favor to those who have heard him preach previously. It was Esskew who baptized Alfonso Marquez in 2010.

While welcoming Christ into his life, Marquez has settled down in his family situation. He moved in recent years with Staci and their toddler son from Orange County to Gilbert, Ariz., a Phoenix suburb easily accessible both to the larger Sky Harbor and ancillary Gateway airports. The move enabled him to see his children from the first marriage – Alfonso, 24; Makeyla, 15; and Christian, 13 – who live in Southern California. It also has allowed the relocated couple to golf, go tandem motorcycle riding, attend 20-plus Phoenix Coyotes' National Hockey League (NHL) games every winter, and be close to the half-dozen MLB spring training sites in the Valley of the Sun.

Wait a minute! This breaks every tired entry in the Book of Stereotypes. A *baseball* umpire, born *south* of the border, going ga-ga for a sport dominated by players from *north* of the border? Just simply does not make sense, you say. It cannot be the mascot – Coyote, same as those "guest escorts" for undocumented workers headed to *El Norte* – or can it?

Let Fonzy Marquez explain why he has ice on his brain so often when away from ball yards: "Most of the NHL referees and linesmen are friends of mine. It goes back to 2000," he said, when the current Washington Nationals still were the Montreal Expos, who played in Olympic Stadium, a relic from the 1976 Summer Games. "I was with (fellow umpire) Brian O'Nora. Montreal and Boston were playing a playoff game" in the Forum, not far from the umpires' hotel.

After the hockey game, Marquez and O'Nora introduced themselves to the three NHL officials who had just finished working. When the hockey game-callers realized exactly who their surprise visitors were, they no longer felt tired, and treated the diamond duo to dinner.

Said Marquez: "We've been very good friends" from that night forward, especially with the surviving two of the three NHL officiating aces, linesmen Jay Sharrers, a Jamaican-born resident of British Columbia, and Andy McElman. McElman, an American from the Chicago suburbs who is in his mid-50s, announced before the 2015-2016 campaign that it would be his last after 23 seasons.

The third new NHL friend was another linesman, Stephane Provost, who was not wearing a safety helmet when he died in a fiery motorcycle crash in South Florida in 2005. Ever since, in Provost's memory, Alfonso Marquez, when he can, carries in his luggage the numbered jersey (hockey people call it a sweater) his late buddy wore on the ice, and hangs it in his umpire locker wherever he is working.

"We've learned a lot from each other. They're such good men," the major leagues' first Mexican-born baseball umpire said, when interviewed exclusively for this book in January 2016. "I try to model myself after them, even though we are working completely different sports. The lifestyle is the same."

Well, kinda, sorta, but not exactly.

"Actually, we always thought we had it bad," on the road in a 162-game regular season, in which MLB umpires work an average of 135-140 games when four weeks paid vacation is subtracted.

"They do three games in three different cities on three different days," an astounded Marquez said. "These guys change after every single game, every single day," he kept muttering to himself.

Marquez discovered as well that he and Sharrers shared another commonality. Sharrers, like Marquez, is an ethnic pioneer – the first-ever black NHL linesman or referee when he debuted in 1990. Sharrers is five years older than Marquez.

***

As much as he always will remember his father's admonition about never forgetting one's roots, Marquez nonetheless has a special place in his heart for his adopted country, and what it has meant to the success he has earned. This applies across-the-board to every member of his family – all of whom originally arrived here via the undocumented route, but have all become naturalized U.S. citizens.

"I love this country," he once told a newspaper reporter. "We've always said it is the country of opportunities. What better example than me?"

A veteran youth league umpire named Ken Avey provided the fire underneath the nascent "rocket" that was teen-aged Alfonso Marquez, unknowingly launching the first stage of a meteoric career flight.

In a PONY League game in Fullerton, when Marquez was 14, he was called out by Avey, who soon realized he had "eaten" the call, as umpires would put it. Rather than lose his temper, the player soon noticed the calmness and contrite manner of the umpire who had made the kind of human error that Men in Blue rarely make.

Marquez's innate curiosity led him into a postgame discussion with Avey. The veteran official, obviously impressed by the young man's reaction in a potentially negative and explosive situation, invited him to explore, then join, a local group that trained and provided umpires for amateur recreational league games. Although the players were mostly young and all unpaid, the activity provided Alfonso Marquez a vehicle for which he could earn pocket money while learning about human nature and the values of patience and good judgment. However, equally as important, it eventually became a life-changing experience.

"I was the youngest in the group by at least 10 years," said Marquez, who went on to officiate youth and recreational league games for six years, before borrowing enough money from an uncle to help cover tuition – $3,700 – to attend the same Florida umpire school where he later would be an instructor. Most of the tuition seed money, though, came from a worker's comp settlement Marquez had won after he almost lost a finger in a machine accident working in a subsistence job.

Although an on-field athletic official's life is a routine rife with anonymity and one for which loved ones do not usually rush to watch you, by the time Marquez had ascended through the minor leagues, his first-ever taste of The Show was literally in his own backyard.

Consequently, his whole family, plus several friends and neighbors, were there to watch him work an annual preseason game in April 1997 between the Los Angeles Dodgers and the Los Angeles Angels of Anaheim at Angel Stadium of Anaheim. It was barely five miles from the Marquez family home in Fullerton. Also in the crowd was an old local *Blue Hombre* friend and fellow Brinkman Umpire School alumnus, Anaheim Police Department polygraph examiner Vincent "Vince" Delgado; a promising minor league umpiring career ended at age 25 in the late '80s when a ball hit Delgado in the head, aggravating a concussive brain battered by previous batted balls hit so hard directly into his face mask that they bent the steel bars. Delgado has worked a side job for years as an MLB Resident Security Agent at the Anaheim ballpark.

***

Alfonso Marquez did not have to venture much farther a little more than two years later when the call came to do his initial *real* regular season game. This time, it was only 65 miles on an interstate highway, but seemingly light-years away – without ever leaving the state of Colorado. The "call" was somewhat of a religious experience, akin to the kind of calling a clergyman receives from the Almighty – only this one, even though the clouds parted, was not from God but merely a National League umpire supervisor, on an off-and-on rainy evening, Aug. 12, 1999. Marquez was working a Triple-A Pacific Coast League (PCL) contest at Security Service Field, home of the Colorado Springs Sky Sox, then the Colorado Rockies' top farm club, on the east side of the picturesque city at the foot of 14,110-foot Pikes Peak, often referred to as America's Mountain.

As the story goes, he was instructed to report for the second half of an NL interdivisional day-night, split doubleheader the next day at Denver's Coors Field between the Rockies and the Montreal Expos. The early start was scheduled for 12:35 p.m., with Marquez slated to do the plate in the "nightcap," starting at 7:05 p.m. – *on Friday* the *13th*. If neither the cloud scenario the previous night nor that date associated with demonic doings were not ominous signs in their own right for a rookie umpire working his first regular season game, nothing was.

Marquez would watch the first game of the split twin bill from a television monitor in the Coors Field clubhouse, anxiously biding time, then spend a few minutes after the contest ended, shortly after 5 p.m., going up to the playing field on a quick guided tour by veteran Crew Chief Jerry Crawford. They talked about the set of potential problems presented by the spacious stadium, situated at a mile-high altitude, but nearly a thousand feet lower than the 6,000-foot elevation in Colorado Springs the evening before.

In a quirk unique to the sport, the day-night split resulted from a rainout earlier in the season between the two teams, causing double indemnity for sufferers of triskaidekaphobia, or fear of the number 13. The fourth regular member of the umpiring crew in Denver, Tony Randazzo, had been originally scheduled, with Crawford and his other crew partners, Paul Nauert and Phil Cuzzi, to do the 7:05 start. However, when Randazzo was granted an authorized absence, he worked the early rainout replay instead, leaving the nighttime slot open for Marquez's call-up from Triple-A.

To avoid potential snags, right after Marquez's PCL game had ended late Thursday night, he had retrieved his two traveling bags, checked out from his hotel, bid *adieu* to his two most recent minor league partners and headed north in a rental car on the hour-plus drive.

Following a good night's sleep at a hotel only blocks from Coors Field, it seems, Marquez had a reasonably authentic, early breakfast of *huevos rancheros* at a popular Lower Downtown Mexican place across from the hotel with his new umpiring partners; there were Crawford – whose father, Shag, had preceded him years before as a big league umpire, and whose younger brother, Joey, still was a longtime National Basketball Association referee – Cuzzi and Nauert, like Marquez, call-ups that same season but already having worked at the top. As was the ritual, Fonzy Marquez, the new kid on the MLB umpiring block, was entitled to a treat for his first meal at the highest possible achievement level with his three cohorts. Fittingly, as the tale can be best recounted, when the waitress placed the tab discreetly in the middle of their table, Cuzzi and Nauert almost butted heads reaching for the paper to shove it towards Crawford, the senior in the group who would pay for Marquez's breakfast.

When a 10-inning, 14-13 slugfest won by Montreal, and having lasted more than four hours, finally ended, Marquez continued to psyche-up himself for his debut in The Show less than two hours later. He also had the pregame presence to ask a clubhouse attendant to prepare a small tub of water with lots of ice – for his postgame routine to soothe swollen feet that would develop from several hours of alternately standing, squatting and bouncing out, along either baseline or into the infield grass, on scores of various plays.

During the slightly shorter-than-normal, two-hour, 48-minute nightcap, Alfonso Marquez might have thought he was working in a junkyard inventorying auto parts. Except for some potential, occasional 95-mile-an-hour "heat" from Montreal starter Javier Vasquez, a 23-year-old Puerto Rican lefthander nicknamed "Silent Assassin," and Expo closer Ugueth Urbina, the eight pitchers – four for each side – combined for only five strikeouts, again far below the norm for a nine-inning major league contest. Instead, the outs made were from a slew of groundouts, lineouts and pop-ups precipitated by an ongoing assortment from each hurler that included every imaginable variation of curves, change-ups and the like – in other words, a "junk" fest.

The hard-hitting host team, known as the Blake Street Bombers, went ahead, 2-1, after one inning – during which a euphoric Marquez had yet to descend from Cloud Nine, still not convinced he was *here*. The Expos eventually pulled out the win, 8-6, to complete the sweep.

"I don't think I remember the first two innings," he recalled to a reporter several years later. "I was nervous, I was excited, I was happy, and on top of all that, I had to call the game." Because he never mentioned it was Friday the 13th, he probably did not realize it anyway. So much for supposed superstition, then.

***

The next evening, Saturday, saw a game eerily similar to the one the night before, only with the home team prevailing in nine innings, 11-8. There was an exact-same number of total strikeouts (5), with all six pitchers (three each side) "dropping a lot of deuces and changes again," as one major league advance scout, sitting behind home plate, put it, referring to a second consecutive outing full of death-defying breaking pitches and off-speed offerings. Marquez had rotated clockwise to cover third base, with Crawford at second, Randazzo having returned from a game's absence at first, and Eric Gregg calling balls and strikes. (Gregg, a huge man who battled weight issues for years, was the third African-American MLB umpire following Emmett Ashford and Art Williams, and died from a stroke in 2006.)

Fonzy Marquez still was hanging around with the big boys on Aug. 15, with the Expos also remaining in Denver. The occasion was to complete a rare, five-game series in another rainout-induced doubleheader, this time played back-to-back in a pair of games that lasted a total of just over five hours. In one more mix-and-match, or maybe "musical chairs," combination involving components of the same umpire crew, the first-game line-up read: Nauert, home plate; Marquez, first base; Randazzo, second base; and Gregg, third base. This weekend-long Blue Chess Game concluded with a clockwise rotation, beginning at the plate, of Randazzo, Cuzzi, Gregg and Marquez. Colorado's Blake Street Bombers piled up 20 runs to sweep the day and win the series.

By later the same night, he was back to the existent reality – his four-game flirtation with baseball's ultimate "beauty queen" over with. Fittingly, realizing his Fantasy Bubble that just burst actually had been temporarily a *genuine* globe-shaped planet on which he floated, within hours, he was in the air en route to his cute but Plain Jane "girlfriend," the Pacific Coast League. Alfonso Marquez returned permanently as an MLB umpire in 2000. Meanwhile, the ever-shifting crew from beer-named Coors Field, and now including Crew Chief Gregg, Nauert, Cuzzi and Brian Gorman, had moved on to the Astrodome for a series pitting the host Astros against another "suds"-dubbed entity, the Milwaukee Brewers, who played their home schedule in brew-themed Miller Park.

***

When one is accustomed to accomplishing a duty he tackles every four or five days in three hours each turn, it can seem like an eternity if an extra hour or more is added on, after the fact.

Such was the case for MLB umpire Alfonso Marquez in what would wind up as the deciding Game 5 of the 2015 World Series at Citi Field in a prime-time Sunday night matchup telecast to hundreds of millions worldwide, and no doubt translated into more languages than one could count on Marquez's ball-strike clicker. The invading Kansas City Royals won the best-of-seven Series, 4-1, by scoring five runs in the top of the 12th inning to break a 2-2 tie. They held the New York Mets scoreless in the bottom half on the way to sealing a 7-2 victory and their first world championship in 30 years.

Having called more than 400 pitches from a total of nine hurlers – four for KC, five for New York – in a contest that lasted four hours and 15 minutes, all the native of Mexico had to do on the final pitch from Royals' closer Wade Davis was to squat just once more in The Box stance and watch with a 1-2 count, two outs and Michael Conforto on at second base. Davis completed striking out the side in his one inning of work, as Mets' batter Wilmer Flores froze, going down looking with the third strike whizzing past him on a 92-mile-per-hour change-up. Marquez paused an extra second, ensuring the ball was in the mitt of KC back-up catcher Drew Butera, who finished backstop duties for the series' Most Valuable Player and Flores's fellow Venezuelan, catcher Salvador Perez. Marquez added the final exclamation point with his emphatic, leg-kicking, "bow-and-arrow" move – coupled with a deep, throaty *"H-e-e-e-y-e-e-e!"* – signifying a called third strike.

Butera, thus, became a second-generation world champion; his father, Sal, had been the most prominent of three rotating catchers (along with Tim Laudner and Tom Nieto) when the elder Butera's Minnesota Twins defeated the St. Louis Cardinals in the 1987 World Series.

Amazingly, Fonzy Marquez lasted all those hours and innings this time, through all those pitches – enough to make a math professor dizzy with each ensuing multiple of permutations and combinations – without major incident or any ball or strike call seriously questioned by either side, as all of baseball's "global village" was watching.

As far as the 16-season MLB veteran was concerned, it was just another "day at the office," the identical way he has approached it every fourth day since the New Millennium dawned.

"I felt good. We," he said, purposely using the third-person, representing the entire umpire brotherhood, in that he was their out-front leader, having just successfully completed the toughest assignment in the year's most important setting for all the world to witness, literally. Then, he re-started at the top again: "We have an idea, coming off the field, how we did, or how you did as an individual, as part of the team," down-shifting and narrowing his assessment to the six-man crew that had just completed the 2015 World Series, as opposed to *all* umpires.

"You have to stay level. I walk away feeling I did a good job. You don't look back. Nobody cares what you did yesterday," he said philosophically. Marquez equated after-the-fact baseball tales with "war stories" – the farther you get beyond their actual occurrence, the more interesting they sound, truth be damned.

*****

With all the psychological and mental aspects associated with good athletic officiating on the field in an increasingly complex society, modern, well-rounded umpires like Marquez also quietly employ a holistic approach. This is wise, from a standpoint of total awareness, even when one is focused like a laser on the game itself.

Police and other security officials – like Marquez's old friend and former *Blue Hombre* Vince Delgado, back in Anaheim – are constantly on alert for spontaneous crowd disruptions, such as a singular drunken patron or fans engaging in fistfights. However, the unsavory events that chill umpires' spines the most are the sudden, unpleasant or even dangerous kind that spill over onto the field of play; they involve the ever-lurking possibility of potentially serious injury, or even death, perpetrated by some unhinged individual or group (think terrorists) whose behavior goes far beyond the average raucous, partisan fan.

"You don't have to have a body-builder's physique, but I keep myself in good physical shape," said Marquez, who works out at local fitness centers wherever his crew is doing a series. He is destined before too long to become a crew chief; he began the 2016 season on a foursome where he was second in seniority only to his new crew chief, longtime veteran Larry Vanover. The other two on the crew were veteran Chris Guccione, who also was baptized by Pastor Dean, and David Rackley, the least seasoned of the four, having made his MLB debut in a brief 2013 call-up. They formed an eclectic group, age- and experience-wise and geographically. The white-maned Vanover, 60 and with two decades as an MLB umpire, hails from western Kentucky; Guccione, a little younger than Marquez at 41 and with similar experience, still lives in the small, scenic south-central Colorado town of Salida, where he was born; and Rackley, the "baby," is 34 and a big-city Texan, originally from Houston, but now residing in Charlotte, N. Car.

The Vanover crew was given a vacation the first week of actual play in early April 2016, and didn't begin making regular-season music as a new quartet until a Los Angeles Angels-Oakland Athletics AL West series in Oakland from April 11-13. In that series and season opener for the crew, the crew chief was behind the plate, with Marquez at first base in a 4-1 victory. Then, the next night, the Angels won again, 5-4, erasing an early deficit, as the Mexico native took the plate for the first time, in a game other than spring training and exhibitions, since his spotless, extra-inning effort in the World Series decider five months earlier.

***

If spending 12 innings and four-plus hours, in the deciding Final Act on the sport's biggest stage, was not enough to satisfy baseball's rich annals, just by doing his job again still early in the next season – squatting back there calling balls and strikes – placed Alfonzo Marquez's name, in indelible ink, permanently in the history books, albeit by chance, not choice.

A 5-0 shutout over the visiting Texas Rangers in an AL match-up at Chicago's U.S. Cellular Field on Friday night, April 22, 2016, saw the host White Sox pull off the baseball equivalent of Halley's Comet, or an event that had *never* happened on a big league diamond: MLB's first-ever 9-3-2-6-2-5 triple play, and initial triple-killing of the 2016 season. With no outs and the bases loaded in the top of the seventh inning, the Rangers' Mitch Moreland ripped a screaming liner into right field, as runners Prince Fielder, Adrian Beltre and Ian Desmond all took off, thinking, of course, the quickly sinking baseball would drop in. However, Chisox right-fielder Adam Eaton made a spectacular diving catch – setting the first match to the firecracker that burned the once-in-a-blue-moon new entry forever into the national pastime's ancient archives.

Being the plate umpire with the "sacks full," prior to the momentous play, Marquez already had signaled – needing only both hands, in one fell swoop – to his three crew partners: 1. closed fists (no outs); 2. wiggling thumbs-up (Infield Fly Rule); and 3. pointing down toward the rubberized plate with both hands (he would be staying close to home). Instead, the 40-something plate guy and 60-ish crew chief Vanover, stationed at third, wound up in a workout up and down the third-base stripe – at either end of the sport's version of a *Conga* line. By the time the ball had passed through the hands of all but three Chicago position players – the left- and center-fielders, and the second baseman – and resulted in the first two outs, the umpiring pair had been taken on a long "rundown ride" between home and third before third baseman Todd Frazier applied the tag to Fielder for the final out. Marquez made it official with a quick, cursory twist of his again-closed-fisted right wrist, Frazier having chased the portly, second-generation major-leaguer back toward home plate into Marquez's "sector" of responsibility.

***

As he consequently creeps ever closer to "chief" status, Fonzy Marquez wants to project to fellow umpires not only acquired wisdom and baseball knowledge, but *that look*. He already is a good example in his physical appearance when each game begins – well-pressed shirt and pants, highly shined shoes, effective but not too flashy protective gear, and well-trimmed hair, including no mustache or beard (except during that period in 2009 when injuries shelved him). Of course, as most games progress, that dapper demeanor is transformed into a collection of grass-stained, dirt-marred clothes and scuffed shoes, and perhaps a small stubble emerging on one's chin.

As mentioned in Chapter 2, 25-year American League veteran Rich Garcia, later an umpire supervisor as Marquez advanced up the ladder in the 21st century's first decade, rated the current Arizonan as among baseball's top arbiters. Also included on Garcia's list of present-day "elites" are the retired operative's longtime ex-crew mate, John Hirschbeck, Bill Miller, Ron Kulpa, Mike Everitt and Vic Carapazza, Garcia's son-in-law but an impressive young umpire still in his 30s.

"I think Fonzy is excellent, excellent," Garcia exclaimed, compelled to repeat himself to emphasize his esteem for the hard-working Marquez, whose first NL season coincided with Garcia's final AL campaign in 1999.

As a group, Garcia added, "these are the guys who understand the game, how to be good umpires. They adjust to situations … don't fall into traps" during the average nine innings and three hours it takes to complete a major league game.

Garcia, whose job it was to evaluate MLB umpires as a supervisor from 2003-2009, singled out some of those "situations" facing contemporary arbiters:

- "**Strategy**. Coping from one manager to the next;
- "**Always watch the ball**, keep your eye on it, of course … but don't turn your back on the field until it's done;
- "**See who throws helmets**, who throws hats down – little psychological things you learn to pick up on."

Garcia said Marquez and the other five modern umpires he cited epitomize what is expected regarding on-field comportment, overall attitude, rules knowledge and application, and general good judgment.

As a crew chief his last 15 seasons in The Bigs, Garcia said he "always tried to do that," the *that* being the *"it"* required to succeed – following the basics and keeping a cool head.

A longtime current MLB crew chief, Gerry Davis, concurred with Garcia's gushing praise of Marquez, saying, "Fonzy's one of our top umpires. He does an awesome job. He has an impressive future ahead of him," provided he can avoid an injurious year like 2009.

Davis added that – for whatever set of reasons – the big leagues began the 2016 season with more umpire injuries "than normal, so early in the year," causing regular crew spots to be filled by eager young talent working in the two Triple-A leagues; while the fill-ins always are anxiously awaiting a decent shot in The Show, they realize, at least subconsciously, *they* could be the injured ones.

***

One other little nuance accomplished by umpires, depending on personal preference, is keeping salivated and hydrated. Among the preferred solutions for guys who never are able to sit or generally have no time for a "potty break" for upwards of three hours or more:

- **Seeds** – Most popular are sunflower seeds, with pumpkin seeds a distant second. Some umpires, like everyone else down on a ball diamond who may be seed fanatics, keep a bag planted deep in a back pocket of the ever-dwindling supply as the game proceeds.

- **Chewing gum** – A couple of sticks of one's favorite flavor will help for a few innings, supplanted by a fresh refill once or twice. Regular bubble gum is employed infrequently because there is too much temptation to blow huge bubbles, thus rendering a base umpire's desired anonymity as compromised. The man behind the plate *never* would even consider sticky bubble gum, knowing full-well that, the first time he was inclined to inflate a globular work of art, it would pop all over the inside of his protective mask.

- **Thirst-quenching gum** – There are two or three most popular brands, all of which serve the salivation role in a similar way to special, flavored thirst-quenching beverages, by replenishing glucose and preventing the "cotton-mouth" effect.

- **Tobacco dipping** – Since smoking, naturally, is banned on big league fields, both officials and players alike can get a dual "buzz" – nicotine and slaking thirst – by placing "a pinch between the cheek and gums," as the old television spot encouraged, of small, moist bits of chewing tobacco, commonly called "dip."

- **The "Big Chaw"** – Look at "ancient" baseball collector cards from the 1940s and '50s, and you'll see many players' faces where one cheek resembles the shape of the bloated tummy of a mother-to-be. What you are actually witnessing is an athlete in a pre-tobacco-is-taboo era proudly posing with a giant "chaw" of chewing *da-backy* filling his cheek.

The chaw discussion was saved for last; it has been the method of choice of Alfonso Marquez for some time in terms of keeping him able to swish the tobacco juice around in his mouth, then allowing the option to lift up his mask and quickly spit out the excess between pitches or when time has been called.

"I tried this out when I first was in the lower minors, and was surprised at how comfortable it was without disrupting my routine," he said. "I was unfortunately still smoking cigarettes to a certain extent away from the ballparks at the time, so it was no big deal. Then, as I stopped smoking for good, I kept increasing the wad in my right cheek, little by little."

With impressionable children always watching, whether in-person or on TV, Marquez has reasoned the time is closer to rid himself of the habit, but he is not quite ready to "toss" the tobacco in the trash can permanently for now.

(*"Psst! Over here."* The imaginary little gnome who hangs around ball diamonds is trying to grab the author's attention. *"Why didn't you tell them about the plastic water bottle umpires tuck up at the bottom of the backstop for sips between innings?"* Because *you* just did, my unseen friend. Anyway, at every MLB venue, there are reliable, in-game batboys who double as pre- and post-game clubhouse attendants, like four-year veteran Ryan Froistad at Denver's Coors Field, who help slake the three base umpires' thirst every 2-3 innings. Froistad, 25, is stationed during Rockies' contests on the top step of the visitors' dugout, ready to sprint onto the field with water bottles for the offing; he confided that many plate umpires spurn his thirst-quenching offers, thus lending credence to the imaginary gnome's contention about the backstop bottle stash.)

***

The small, rock-strewn field in the southern part of Zacatecas state is a distant memory. Yet despite that, it remains forever in the psyché of Alfonso "Fonzy" Marquez – as long as guys like him, Ted Barrett and Jorge Bauzá, resembling Magi, keep returning there, and also to such places as Monterrey, Mexico City and Guadalajara. Instead of ancient, biblical gifts of *frankincense* and *myrrh*, though, these three wise men only want to bring shin guards, chest protectors, masks, safety shoes and even balls, bats and gloves.

6

MANNY GONZALEZ
'MR. PERSONALITY' LETS IT SHINE

It is a pleasant, midsummer evening on Aug. 6, 2013, in the Big Apple – Flushing Meadows-Corona Park in the borough of Queens, to be exact. A light breeze wafts through Citi Field, where the visiting Colorado Rockies are facing the New York Mets in the Tuesday opener of a three-game set the Mets would sweep.

With his team trailing, 2-1, in the top of the sixth inning, Colorado's left-hand-swinging Charlie Blackmon, pinch-hitting for starting pitcher Chad Bettis, steps in to the right-side batter's box to lead off. On the first pitch from Mets right-handed starter Jennry Mejia, Blackmon offers at the ball and makes contact on a bunt attempt. But the baseball bounces quickly into foul territory directly behind the plate, ricocheting straight between the jaw and Adam's apple of plate umpire Manny Gonzalez. The ball has found a vulnerable place – "a not-so-sweet spot" – left unprotected by the umpire's space-age, hard-plastic, hockey-goalie-style, supposedly "protective" headgear called The Tube.

For a split-second, the sudden contact stuns the first-ever Major League Baseball umpire from Venezuela, 33 years old at the time. Despite the impact, Gonzalez remains erect momentarily, then involuntarily falls to the ground with a contrite Blackmon standing astride his left side attempting to console him. The crowd of 27,198 collectively gasps, amid the roar of jets overhead taking off or about to land at nearby La Guardia airport, in the Mets' home park that had replaced adjacent, four-decades-old Shea Stadium in 2009.

It takes 17 minutes to tend to Gonzalez, lying still in the exact spot where he went down. Fortunately, as a Mets' team doctor continues to treat him inside the clubhouse, pronouncing him "fine," play has resumed, minus one of the four umpires; silver-maned veteran Larry Vanover moves from second base to replace Gonzalez calling balls and strikes, while Tony Randazzo and Crew Chief Brian Gorman, the latter a second-generation big league umpire with white hair rivaling Vanover's, share the bases, staying at the "corners." Texan David Rackley is called up from the AAA International League (IL) for the first time as a professional umpire to fill Gonzalez's slot for the crew's next assignment.

***

Sufficiently rested and rehabilitated, Manny Gonzalez rejoins Brian Gorman's crew on Aug. 26, one day short of three weeks following the injury, hooking up with Gorman, Randazzo and a new "fourth," Colorado native Cory Blaser. Blaser, then 31, had broken into the majors in April 2010, a month preceding his new, returning Venezuela-bred crew-mate's debut in a May 17 contest at Sun Life Stadium in suburban Miami Gardens between the host Florida (now Miami) Marlins and the Arizona Diamondbacks. Blaser had learned the rudiments of the craft from his dad, Bob, a longtime, well-respected college umpire.

(On that spring day three years earlier, Gonzalez covered third base in his MLB "baptism of fire." The others in his initial group were late Crew Chief Wally Bell, who died of a heart attack in October 2013 after having called his final game, at first base; Laz Díaz, another *Blue Hombre*, at second; and James Hoye behind the plate. Upon his death, in both the AL and NL league championship series that immediately ensued, all of Bell's umpiring colleagues honored his memory by wearing a small, circular, black-and-white sleeve patch emblazoned with the initials, "WB.")

On the 2013 Gorman-led crew, Blaser has replaced Vanover, who moved to a different foursome, while Rackley has gone back down to the IL, having now become "one of those up-and-down guys" referred to often by minor league umpiring *guru* Jorge Bauzá. A Triple-A umpire with up-and-down status is one designated to move quickly – sometimes with just a few hours' notice as a temporary call-up – to replace a big league regular who may be ill, injured, using paid vacation time, or has been granted an excused absence for other personal reasons.

In this case, the venue is indoors at domed Chase Field in downtown Phoenix, an NL West night game to open a three-game series between the home-standing Diamondbacks and the San Diego Padres. (Many Arizona fans were disappointed when the retractable-roofed stadium's original owner of naming rights, Bank One of Chicago, merged with larger JPMorgan Chase, in 2005, effecting the change to a blander handle that did not lend itself to a catchy nickname. The popular acronymic moniker for Bank One Ballpark was "The BOB" – appropriate for an indoor ball yard replete with beach balls and a swimming pool beyond the center-field fence.)

Gonzalez is assigned home plate as a "welcome back" gift, and enjoys a relatively uncomplicated outing, considering he easily could have died or been turned into a "vegetable" less than a month earlier if a bat-propelled baseball had hit him mere inches higher than his neck or jawbone and had knocked off his supposedly futuristic headgear in the process. His return assignment lasts only 2½ hours, a half-hour less than the MLB norm, and he looks at a total of only 254 pitches by both pitching staffs, which averages out to only about 25 pitches per inning – meaning many batters are putting balls into play early in the count. From a modern-day Sabermetrics standpoint, this conclusion is borne out by the fact all pitchers that evening combine for only 15 strikeouts, and only four batters walk, all courtesy of the three Padres hurlers.

***

Tuesday, Oct. 6, 2015, marked a genuine New Dawn in the life and professional progression of 36-year-old Manny Gonzalez. While he was not required to rise for an evening's worth of work until much later in the day, the Venezuelan-turned-Floridian was anxious to awaken as early as possible in his Midtown Manhattan hotel; the 6-foot, 210-pounder wanted to do a quick workout in the hotel fitness center before joining his five "business" partners, all older than he was, for a hearty breakfast in the first-floor café.

Their next cooperative assignment would be that evening at 8 o'clock as the umpiring crew for the American League Wild Card Game; it was a one-and-done scenario matching the surprising AL West runner-up Houston Astros and the New York Yankees, who placed second behind Toronto in the AL East Division.

As was the case with most MLB umpire crews, here stood a fairly eclectic bunch – a dream collection of humanity for any anthropologist or similar scientific researcher – in its ethnic, experience, geographic and personality distribution. Other than Gonzalez, who was assigned Right Field, those in this six-man group scheduled to work the Wild Card game at the third incarnation of the twice-thoroughly-remodeled House That Ruth Built – Yankee Stadium III, as it was now called – were all in their 40s, and they included:

- **Eric Cooper**, age 48, Home Plate: A burly Iowan best known for firing new baseballs back to pitchers, rather than the more common practice of letting the catcher perform that chore; he debuted as an AL arbiter in 1999;

- **Paul Emmel**, 48, First Base: Holder of a B.A. degree in Finance from Central Michigan University; the intensely quiet Emmel, whose first big league game was in the NL in 1999, worked the plate on May 6, 2012, when Texas Ranger Josh Hamilton tied the all-time, single-game record with four home runs against the Baltimore Orioles;

- **Ted Barrett**, 50, Second Base: A gregarious, 6-foot-4, 255-pound ordained minister who earned multiple college and theological degrees (as detailed in Chapter 5), and crew chief since 2013; the most-experienced member of this crew first was an AL umpire in 1994;

- **Bill Miller**, 48, Third Base: A high-strung California native, named an MLB crew chief in 2014, after breaking in as an AL umpire in 1997; Miller, a non-Latino, earned a History degree from UCLA; he also is cited by the longest-serving Latino umpire in MLB annals,

Rich Garcia, as arguably one of the sport's top half-dozen umpires, along with John Hirschbeck, Ron Kulpa, Alfonso Marquez, Mike Everitt and Vic Carapazza.

- **Chris Conroy**, 41, Left Field. The next-youngest crew member after Gonzalez, he hails from Massachusetts and, like the Venezuelan, had his major league debut in 2010, was hired to the full-time staff three seasons later, and the 2015 AL Wild Card marked his inaugural postseason work; Conroy was one of three MLB umpires selected in November 2014 for the MLB Japan All-Star Series.

When the game finally was under way, Astros right-hander and 2015 AL Cy Young Award winner Dallas Keuchel, resembling the Depression Era barnstorming House of David nine with his apt-for-this-occasion, wild, flowing beard, and three relievers who followed him, combined for a three-hit, 3-0 shutout in the one-game-and-done playoff. That enabled Houston to advance to the AL Divisional Series, where the Astros were eliminated by ultimate World Series champion Kansas City, three games to two.

In the Astros-Yankees Wild Card contest, played on a beautiful, slightly breezy, 67-degree autumn night in the South Bronx, Manny Gonzalez's activity down the line in right field was limited mostly to signifying fair, foul or out on several line drives or pop flies in his specific sector. That was the routine on batter after batter following a second-inning, leadoff home run by Houston's Colby Rasmus deep to right, which meant the umpire had to hustle into fair territory on that play; he signaled "home run" by extending his right arm high into the air while simultaneously twirling his right wrist and pointing skyward with his index finger.

***

"He's like a son to me. I'm extremely proud of him. I saw him growing up," said Bauzá of Gonzalez. The former himself "grew up" observing many games as a youth at ballparks such as San Juan's Hiram Bithorn Stadium in his native Puerto Rico. Bauzá, a former 11-year minor league umpire and now the chief field evaluator for Minor League Baseball (MiLB) and the organization's primary pursuer of Latin American umpiring talent, was half-kidding with the father-son reference. At 46, he is barely a decade senior to Manny Gonzalez, yet the two have developed at least an older-younger-brother relationship.

"When he first came to us, he was shy – inside a shell," the 15-year veteran of evaluating MiLB umpires, present and future, said of Gonzalez, whose given name is Manuel Augusto Gonzalez. "He was thinking too much. Then, he came out of the shell."

Bauzá was implying that Gonzalez, the highest achiever thus far among the many officiating prospects he has mentored, actually is a "natural umpire" and "Mr. Personality." When the current MLB umpire's "personality came out, the confidence came out" with it, Bauzá added. Gonzalez, he said, "... had that X-factor that not a lot of people have." Bauzá's comments exclusively for this book were compiled in a series of interviews between December 2015 and May 2016.

The evaluator/field instructor also described Manny Gonzalez as one of the most diligent persons he has ever known.

Gerry Davis, MLB's second-most-senior umpire, and a longtime crew chief, agreed with Bauzá's assessment of the Venezuelan pacesetter. "Any time you go to a foreign country, you're reserved," Davis surmised in response during interviews, also specifically for this book, between April and June 2016. When Gonzalez was a member of his crew for some games in 2015, the soft-spoken, yet firmly situated, veteran of thousands of major league contests said he noticed the younger umpire was "a quick study" and simply a keen student of the game whose shining personality became apparent.

Coming to umpire school in a new country after arriving in Florida from the rolling plains of his picturesque South American homeland – amply spread between the Andes peaks and Caribbean waves, and bisected by the Orinoco River – did indeed cause some early hesitancy for the normally outgoing Gonzalez.

Yet, this eager, 30-something "pup," among a kennel of dozens of snarling, growling, typically skeptical "old dogs," mostly ranging in age from mid-40s to mid-60s, held his own, and kept smiling, rather than turn himself into a raging pit bull.

"Manny had a lot of experience in the leagues down there," and it was evident in his performance, said Davis, whose calm demeanor would more likely place him, in a second, "dog's life," as perhaps an avuncular St. Bernard or large sheepdog, rather than among the more vicious breeds.

Under the additional guidance of former 25-year American League umpire Rich Garcia, Gonzalez earned a scholarship, then completed umpire school with high ratings, indicating that success loomed heavily in his future.

Gonzalez was able to fulfill his desire of wearing No. 79 on his uniform, denoting his birth year of 1979, similar to the step taken by several others including *Blue Hombres* colleagues, No. 72, Mexico native Alfonso Marquez, who was born seven years before him, and No. 63, Laz Díaz, born in 1963 in Miami.

***

As the 2016 regular season kind of limped out of the starting gate, lame-racehorse style, with openers in several of the 15 scheduled series either postponed or delayed by nasty weather, Manny Gonzalez latched on to the crew helmed by Fieldin Culbreth, along with CB Bucknor and Jim Reynolds, one of his crew-mates in the 2015 AL Wild Card game. Their first series together in 2016 featured two AL East rivals, the Baltimore Orioles and Boston Red Sox, squaring off at Fenway Park to begin the second week on April 11. The Culbreth crew sat out Week 1, having been granted an opening week's non-traditional paid vacation, similar to that of the Larry Vanover crew.

In the opener at the storied Beantown ballpark, as was customary, Crew Chief Culbreth, the South Carolinian whom everyone knows as "Cubby," grabbed the plate. Gonzalez, fourth in seniority, was assigned third base, with Reynolds at second and Bucknor at first. The very windy afternoon resulted in the lead see-sawing, as the visitors posted three runs in the top of the ninth inning to win, 9-7, and remain unbeaten at 6-0. Gusts exceeding 20 miles per hour forced most fly balls to the opposite field, so Gonzalez did not have to angle-out much into left field, toward Fenway's fabled "Green Monster," except on a couple of line drives.

The second meeting in the three-game series was at night – 7:10 on Tuesday, April 12 – making the next morning perfect for a few extra, rare sleep-in "winks." Downtown hotels like this one in old colonial cities such as Boston usually had enough spacious higher-floor rooms to afford umpires quiet comfort far up from the urban traffic noise that invaded the lower lodgings. Perhaps the young Venezuelan was expecting something to happen later at Fenway because after waking up and downing a hearty breakfast, Gonzalez worked out briskly in the hotel's exercise room – just as he had in preparing for that Wild Card contest in New York.

Once back on the old diamond, Baltimore posted another 9-spot en route to a 9-5 victory, the wind having subsided considerably, leaving the Orioles with seven straight triumphs to start the 2016 season. In the top of the eighth inning, it *happened* – that one play providing the extra adrenaline jag Manny Gonzalez seemed somehow to be instinctively anticipating. As the inning began, he lined up, as usual, behind the second-base bag in short center field. Then, with lanky left-handed-hitting Ryan Flaherty at the plate and a 1-0 count, the 6-foot-3 jack-of-all-trades slapped a screaming-Mimi, low line drive off of Boston right-handed reliever Robbie Ross, just past Gonzalez on its way to deep center. The alert umpire did a *pirouette*, Baryshnikov-style, and spun around to sprint back in toward the infield to ready himself for a close tag play, as Red Sox center-fielder Jackie Bradley, Jr., quickly chased down the ball, whipping it back in bull's-eye fashion to a waiting Xander Bogaerts at second.

Was Cubby Culbreth's newest, youngest crew-mate *really*, deep-down, wishing for such a play? Well, if so, the genie granted the wish, as Flaherty barreled into the base and, with a perfect angle and look, Gonzalez loudly called out the runner on Bogaerts's sweeping tag. To which O's Manager Buck Showalter – no doubt wanting to pad a 9-4 lead – challenged the call, forcing a video review by the boys in the big suite at 945 Park Ave. in the Big Apple. Ol' Buck was spurned, though – *"Upon further review"* – by the New York bunch, who upheld Manny Gonzalez's mechanically correct, well-timed rulebook-perfect call.

The evening after that, the "getaway" game, found Boston snapping the Orioles' unbeaten string, 4-2, thus salvaging a series win, with Gonzalez at first base.

By mid-May 2016, in light of the unusually heavy spate of injuries besetting MLB umpiring crews mentioned by Gerry Davis, Manny Gonzalez found himself with Crew Chief Jeff Nelson, Gonzalez's fellow *Blue Hombre* Díaz and young umpiring prospect Ben May for a three-game series at Arlington's Globe Life Park pitting the host Texas Rangers against the Chicago White Sox. Just a few weeks earlier in Chicago, the South Side Sox had pulled off that historic "Halley's Comet," 9-3-2-6-2-5 triple play on Texas, prominently involving *Blue Hombre* plate umpire Marquez, after the Rangers had loaded the bases with no outs. Ben May, at 34, was nearly three years Gonzalez's junior. With the same Nelson-led foursome intact, the crew then moved way up north to call a San Diego-at-Milwaukee series.

***

Despite great strides over the years in many regards, there always will be some prejudice against anyone with a Spanish surname. Therefore, subtle, unconscious – even unintended – forms of racism still appear.

For instance, just as Gonzalez was about to do the plate in a San Francisco Giants-Colorado Rockies game at Coors Field on May 28, 2016, a Rockies' radio play-by-play man who is not Latino, announcing umpire positions, said it this way: *"… Here are today's umpires: at home plate, Gabe … er … Manny Gonzalez …"*

This could be regarded as an understandable, innocent *faux pas*, considering the Rockies had just ended an East Coast swing two days before against the Red Sox at Fenway Park, where California born-and-bred Gabe Morales was one of the umpires. Conversely, perhaps it may have offered an underlying hint of the idea in some minds that "they all look alike."

***

At the new season's onset, a small handful of Gonzalez's *Blue Hombres* colleagues were relegated to "up-and-down" status, eligible for quicker call-ups.

Among them were Kentucky resident Roberto Ortiz, a native of Puerto Rico; Ramon de Jesus, from the Dominican Republic; Californians Alex Ortiz (not related to Roberto) and Chris Gonzalez (no relation to Manny); and

111

Texan-turned-Nevadan Albert Ruiz. Until they are called up, each most likely would be working games in the two Triple-A leagues, the Pacific Coast and International. (In late April 2016, de Jesus became the first Dominican Republic native to umpire a regular season game – which is discussed more at length in Chapter 8.)

7

GABE MORALES
YOUNG, BUT PROMISING

At 32 years old, Northern California native Gabe Morales is one of the current crop of promising young umpires – Latino descent or not – who already have worked their fair share of major league games. As the 2016 regular season kicked into gear, he had completed nearly 200 MLB games from 2014 through 2015.

Morales hails from Livermore, an East Bay suburb southeast of Oakland. Athletically, Livermore has not been renowned as a *Blue Hombre* incubator, but rather as the Alameda County city that produced a 2015 first-ballot Baseball Hall of Fame inductee, southpaw pitcher Randy Johnson, a 6-foot-10 specimen popularly known as "The Big Unit." Morales's fellow *Hombre*, Alfonso Marquez, the first Mexican-born MLB umpire, was calling balls and strikes in a March 24, 2001, spring training game in Arizona when a Johnson fastball plunked a bird flying in front of home plate – no doubt triggering some new, avian-related phraseology.

Away from sports, the bedroom community of 80,000-plus population has gained both fame and notoriety. The former niche has been derived from the long-standing presence in the city's southeastern corner of the Lawrence Livermore National Laboratory, a prestigious research facility where government agencies and private contractors have partnered for more than a half-century on numerous top-secret weapons-related projects. In the latter case, material for a 1970 documentary film, *Gimme Shelter*, and an album and single of the same title by England's Rolling Stones resulted from chaos leading to several deaths on Dec. 6, 1969, at the former Altamont Speedway hillside outdoor concert venue, just east of Livermore; members of the notorious Hells Angels motorcycle gang had descended on the site during a Woodstock-like concert, originally as security personnel for the crowd of 300,000-plus, but wound up precipitating, rather than preventing, mass havoc.

***

Gabriel Alejandro Morales had not quite hit age 30 yet when he took his initial bow wearing the blue-and-gray uniform of an MLB umpire, with the No. 47 affixed to his shirt sleeve, just below his right shoulder. Twenty-nine-years old still was considered young to be making calls in The Show. The tableau was not as ominous as the Friday the 13th debut in Denver a few years back of good friend and mentor Alfonso Marquez because Morales's "first date" was the *day after* April Fool's on April 2, 2014. Hence, if the young Northern Californian did not fare well during a twi-night doubleheader, only 22 miles from home, there would be no way to blame it on an April Fool's prank.

The twin bill at the Oakland Coliseum, in which the hometown Athletics and Cleveland Indians split, with Oakland winning the opener, was witnessed by a crowd of 15,134, including several dozen friends and family members from Livermore, only 30 miles from the South Oakland stadium. By the nightcap, though, the number of attendees had shrunk to 12,197.

Part of a crew headed by Mike Winters, Morales was assigned third base in the first game, then moved inside to second base for evening duty. In Game One, Mike Muchlinski was at first base, and Winters at second. Game Two found Wegner retreating to help in a replay review role, as Andy Fletcher came on the field to grab the plate, and Winters and Muchlinski moved, respectively, to first and third.

After a minor league game in 2010, Morales had vowed to a reporter his stated goal was to "keep my nose down and do what I'm told, then I'll be rewarded . . . We're all looking to make it, but at the same time, you never know what could happen."

Like revered senior umpire Gerry Davis had described Venezuelan MLB call-up arbiter Carlos Torres, Morales was dubbed a "quick study" by Jorge Bauzá, Field Evaluator/Instructor, MiLB Umpire Development, and Lead Rules Instructor, MiLB Umpire Training Academy; Bauzá is regarded as somewhat of a *guru* and big brother to up-and-coming prospects, especially a rising Latino core. "These guys are intelligent as a group and as individuals, and they have demonstrated all the traits it takes to be good umpires," Bauzá said.

He also termed the "up-and-down guys" – or those like Morales, Torres and another half-dozen or so umpires who have been experienced operatives shuttling "up and down" to the majors from the minors, and back, without missing a beat – as faithful to the program, dedicated to the game and patient with the system.

A Davis assessment of the San Jose, Calif.-born Morales, was based on a retrospective view to the 2015 regular season when, the old veteran said of the *Blue Hombre*, "I had him on my crew a couple of times as a call-up. He handled himself extremely well."

***

In the fairly short span of less than two seasons in 2014-15, Gabe Morales learned first-hand how mere inches can spell the difference between survival and vulnerability. Two separate incidents underscored these lessons.

The earlier experience was an American League interdivisional night game on July 9, 2014, at Seattle's Safeco Field between the Mariners and the Minnesota Twins.

With Morales behind the plate in the top of the eighth inning and Minnesota easily in front, 8-1, Twins shortstop Eduardo Nuñez battled through nine pitches, forcing a full count by fouling off four offerings from Seattle's Brandon Maurer, before grounding out. But on one swing in the sequence, the right-hand-hitting Nuñez lost control of his bat, which flew straight, barrel-first, to the top-front of Morales's mask, knocking the young arbiter out of his stance. Crew Chief Dale Scott rushed in with the two other base umpires, Lance Barksdale and Kerwin Danley, and, after conferring with the Mariners' trainer, Scott let Morales finish the game's final 1 2/3 innings.

Less than a year later – May 12, 2015 at Phoenix's Chase Field – another interdivisional match-up, this one in the National League, pitted the Washington Nationals against the Arizona Diamondbacks. Two of the members of "Country" Joe West's crew, along with Rob Drake, were Morales and Danley, who was on the "dish." In one of those ongoing ironies that seem common to baseball, with roles switched from the previous season at Seattle and Morales working second base in the bottom of the second inning, Danley absorbed a sharp foul ball off the bat of the D-Backs' Nick Ahmed; this time, however, the shot hit squarely into the umpire's mask.

Danley, forced to leave the game, was taken directly to a local hospital to undergo a CT scan to check for a possible concussion. After having returned to the locker room for a few minutes to re-tool, the three remaining umpires re-emerged, with Morales finishing the rest of the game replacing Danley behind the plate, and West and Drake splitting infield responsibilities from the corners.

That night in downtown Phoenix, all runs for both sides were scored in the first six innings en route to a 14-6 rout by the host squad. Morales looked at 234 pitches after supplanting his wounded crewmate, largely biding his time, particularly in the bottom half of innings 4 through 6, when the D-Backs piled up 11 runs. Yet, with only three umpires, the rock-hard, 6-foot, 185-pounder had to hustle down to make a small handful of calls at third, as Drake raced in from first to cover home plate. Mostly, though, the Northern Californian watched runners touch the plate in pinwheel fashion 20 times in those initial innings.

***

Gabe Morales found the semblance of a permanent home – at least umpire-wise – when the 2016 MLB season kicked off on April 3. He was placed, technically as a call-up, on a crew headed by a wizened, wily veteran crew chief, almost-60 (in September 2016) Kentuckian Tom Hallion. In a season opener in Oakland – in front of, it seemed, half the population of Livermore, similar to two years and a day previously, on the same field – Morales was assigned third base. Filling out the Hallion-led quartet were Phil Cuzzi at second base and Dan Bellino at third. This time, the Chicago White Sox held off the Athletics, 4-3, with all seven runs scored in the busy third inning. After Morales moved over to second base the next day, the result was the same – a one-run Chisox victory, 5-4. However, locals interested in the fate of one specific umpire, as much as wanting Oakland to win, reaped their money's worth on a potentially controversial, "bang-bang" slide play that Morales got 100% right, "selling" the call with his booming voice and arm-leg motion like he was hawking a used car on nearby East 14th Street.

The sweep was averted on April 6, though, when the Athletics held off the visitors, 2-1, in a nationally televised ESPN2 featured contest. With the TV audience – maybe except on the East Coast – staying awake on a Wednesday night until the game ended at past 11 o'clock, Pacific time, the locally bred umpire demonstrated good mechanics at first base; whether hustling to cover a foul pop behind him down the right-field line, getting a good angle to watch a sinking line drive into the right-fielder's glove, or keeping his old "nose down" promise six years later on routine "wide open" out calls at first base, Morales acquitted himself well. And, like most MLB umpires, anyway, the 30-something operative was so skillful that few noticed – *just* the way it is supposed to be when one attains the top tier in his chosen profession.

The four-game Sox-Athletics stand was culminated April 7, as Chicago scored four runs in the top of the ninth inning for a 6-1 victory, cinching a 3-1 series edge. Morales finally got his first taste of plate action in the new season, offering his friends and family – the ones who *did* notice – an early, first-hand look at the determined young man's performance at each regular umpire position. While he kept his nose down even more, focusing on every pitch, Gabe Morales was able to imagine – transcendentally – that he was instead in some stadium far from this one in the county in which he grew up.

***

By late April 2016, Morales, technically still an "itinerant," by MLB assignment standards, at least, and in official status as a call-up/fill-in, had moved for a single series to Jerry Meals's crew, joined there by Paul Nauert and Chris Conroy. However, not yet permanently placed, he soon was replaced by veteran Ron Kulpa – one of those listed among Rich Garcia's Top Six Umps – for one series before re-joining Nauert, Conroy and Kulpa for an April-ending Giants-Mets series in New York, with Meals on an authorized absence. Morales handled home plate in the April 29 opener, a 13-1 laugher won by the New Yorkers.

Shortly thereafter, Meals had returned, and Gabe Morales still was hanging out with him, Kulpa and Conroy in an early May Tigers-Indians tangle at Cleveland's Progressive Field. Then, as all the dizzying crew shuffling continued, he hooked up in Seattle for a Mariners-Tampa Bay Rays series from May 9-11 with a Jerry Layne-led crew that also included veteran Hunter Wendelstedt, owner of an offseason umpire school, and another relative newcomer, Tripp Gibson III. Gibson, who debuted in The Bigs in July 2013 and achieved permanent full-time status in February 2015, was replaced in late May 2016 by Scott Barry. Morales staked claim, albeit temporarily, to his "adopted" status on Layne's crew by remaining despite the official tag as a call-up. In early June 2016, the young Bay Area product also remained when Layne took a week's vacation during an Arizona-Cubs series at Chicago's Wrigley Field.

However, not long thereafter, Morales, a California-born-and-bred Latino, landed on Ted Barrett's crew (first mentioned briefly in Chapter 3), which was much like a United Nations delegation; its components also included: Barrett, a non-Latino and Washington state native now living in Arizona; Angel Hernández, born in Cuba but a South Floridian since childhood; and Stu Scheurwater, the only big league umpire from Canada at the time and, like Morales, a call-up (*Blue Canuck, or Blue Mountie, perhaps?*). In a two-game, interleague sweep of the New York Yankees by the Colorado Rockies at Denver's now-familiar, mile-high Coors Field on June 14-15, the Canadian was assigned third base in Game One, then was replaced by veteran Chris Guccione, who lives in Colorado, in the second game.

Following the two dates in the Rocky Mountain Region, Barrett/Hernández/Morales were joined from June 17-19 in Kansas City by Tennessee-based Will Little for a three-game AL Central slugfest pitting invading Detroit against the defending World Series champion Royals.

As the midseason break for the July 12 All-Star Game rapidly approached, there was an odd occurrence – in a 2-1, 13-inning KC victory, the 3½-hour third game of that series – which matched one dubious milestone with the other. In the top of the 11th, plate umpire Morales ejected Detroit outfielder Cameron Maybin for arguing balls and strikes. The Tiger struck out against Royals reliever Peter Moylan, and seemed to say something to Morales on the batter's slow return toward the dugout. A further, brief exchange ensued, and Maybin was sent showering early. It marked his first major league ejection, and Morales's first in 2016. In reviewing the sequence of pitches during that at-bat, applying the Sabermetrics system, it appeared that every pitch was administered correctly, including the thigh-high offering that crossed within the strike zone sufficiently for Morales to call Maybin out.

In an immediately ensuing series the final week of June 2016 at Cincinnati's Great American Ball Park, Morales kept the integrity of the "M Squad" nickname intact – his last name beginning with the letter M – when he rejoined crew chief Mike Winters, Mike Muchlinski and Marty Foster in a Cubs-Reds set of games.

8

'UP-AND-DOWN' GUYS
THEY HAVE CALL-UP STORIES

Sometimes, success has to be measured in varying degrees. Such has been the case for *Blue Hombres* who nevertheless are able to say, "Been there; done that."

Of course, those who achieved regular, non-fill-in umpiring positions in The Show were Armando Rodriguez, Rich Garcia and the present-day officials: Angel Hernández, Laz Díaz, Alfonso Marquez and Manny Gonzalez.

Then there is that sub-group of younger Latino hopefuls, several of whom have accomplished at least part of their collective dreams by calling balls and strikes in the major leagues. For example, 42-year-old Angel Campos can boast of the longest major league umpiring tenure by far – all or part of eight seasons. However, along with fellow Southern Californian Ramon Armendariz, 43, neither of their contracts in professional baseball was renewed before the 2016 season kicked into gear. If they were to continue umpiring, some of the varied options included college, high school, summer adult leagues or internationally, where some already had broken ground – in Ramon Armendariz's case, Taiwan.

Yet, a Venezuelan in the same boat survived the cut, staying alive to say "hello" to a big league crew in his latest season. Carlos Torres, 37, despite starting out older than most rookie baseball officials, may well be on his way to surpassing Campos's longevity someday following Torres's MLB debut in 2015. In 2016, opening the new season at the top, as part of a four-man crew, put Torres in a better mind-set than being at the Triple-A level.

The 6-foot-3, 218-pounder technically still was not a full-fledged, permanent MLB crew member, but was filling a call-up slot on a crew led by baseball's No. 2 umpire in years served, Gerry Davis. Non-Latinos Rob Drake and Sam Holbrook were the other two on Davis's 2016 crew when the season began. In other words, Torres basically was in the same call-up status as U.S.-born Gabe Morales (subject of this book's Chapter 7.)

"Carlos was one of the guys I wanted. They always ask your opinion," Davis explained, the "they" being umpire supervisors Randy Marsh and Rich Rieker, both retired MLB game-callers. "I actually gave them different names – four or five guys," Davis added when first interviewed for this book in April 2016.

"He's technically very strong," the man who has worked a record number of postseason contests said, describing his take on one who was hoping to work his first playoff game in 2016. "His mechanics are good; timing and knowing the rules – all the attributes you need. He has a lot of experience in Latin America. Carlos does a great job."

The well-seasoned crew chief said that, even though his own Spanish proficiency is limited, Torres conversely has a good command of the English language – meaning no communications problems are anticipated.

"I called some games in Puerto Rico in 1979, so I picked up some Spanish. I can say 'bathroom' and order a cold beer," Davis conceded, never betraying a poker face.

***

While there are men still umpiring in the major leagues well into their 60s, they nonetheless represent the exception. Some, though, have worked either in the American or National leagues, or both, for more than three decades; they include the likes of Davis and Joe West – the latter, like the former, a frequent mentor of Latino colleagues, whether on-field, as an umpire school instructor or in offseason clinics.

It is conceivable that someday, Carlos Torres could equal their staying power. Already in his late 30s, the Venezuelan enjoyed a bite-size taste of MLB umpiring in his initial shot on the top rung of the baseball ladder in 2015, but had spent most of his professional pursuit as a *Blue Hombre* only in infrequent call-up roles during regular season games or spring training contests. Otherwise, the bulk of Torres's baseball officiating existence the past couple of seasons had been in the IL, the main Triple-A feeder for the big leagues along the Eastern Seaboard. That is, until his opening-day assignment to the Davis crew; they officiated the 2016 interleague lid-lifter in Kansas City that paired the New York Mets and World Champion Royals in a rematch of the last previous World Series.

The squads split two games – played April 3 and 5 because of a weather cancellation on April 4. Torres was at third base in Game One, which the Mets won, 4-3, and at second in Game Two, a 2-0 KC shutout.

The second Venezuelan to achieve at least part-time status in the penthouse of his profession, he broke in on July 17, 2015, in an all-Ohio interleague game at Cincinnati's Great American Ballpark featuring the host Reds against the Cleveland Indians. He was at second base on a crew headed by veteran Jeff Kellogg, a good on-field "policeman," with a B.S. degree in criminal justice from Michigan's Ferris State University; another longtime toiler in Ohioan Brian O'Nora, and a promising youngster and future crew mate, Cory Blaser, whose father, Bob, known more familiarly as "Blaze," was a widely respected college umpire for many years in Colorado. Torres was awarded No. 37 (same as his age at the time) – rather unusual since call-ups or other fairly new members of the MLB "Blue Fraternity" typically are assigned numbers in the 70s, 80s or 90s.

The Reds staked themselves to an early 5-0 lead en route to a 6-1 win. The Venezuelan import experienced a healthy variety of activity. The work included being the primary umpire on the front end of three ground-ball double plays, hustling out to deeper center field to determine catch-or-no-catch on a handful of fly balls and line drives, and situating himself at the best angle to watch a solo shot by Cincinnati's Trevor Bauer "leave the yard" in the bottom of the fourth inning.

In 2016, Torres continued his staying power, remaining No. 4 on the Davis crew deep into May with the crew chief and Drake, while Torres' one-time former partner Blaser was inserted in Holbrook's stead. Then, by late that month, the call-up from South America, like his California-born *Blue*

Hombre colleague Morales, maintained ground with Davis, as Blaser shifted to Joe West's crew when Holbrook returned.

The lanky Venezuelan chalked up his first major league ejection in a New York Mets-Colorado Rockies series at Denver's Coors Field on May 14. Working the plate with one out, a 2-2 count and the bases loaded in the bottom of the third inning, Torres quickly and assertively ruled that Colorado batter Tony Wolters nicked the ball on his swing at a rapidly sinking curve by New York's Logan Verrett. However, Mets Manager Terry Collins vehemently disagreed (on a play exempt from instant review) and, when he adamantly refused to relent, the plate umpire sent the skipper to the showers.

More than baseball was on the *Venezolano's* mind that balmy spring evening in Denver because, just the previous day, President Nicolas Maduro had declared a national state of emergency in their homeland. Maduro's action came in the wake of the impeachment of President Dilma Rousseff, his socialist soulmate, in neighboring Brazil; the Venezuelan leader cited the United States as the main culprit triggering his sudden move despite lack of evidence supporting such a broad claim.

With the 2016 MLB campaign having just passed the two-month mark the first week of June, Torres retained his customary coolness and consistency despite moving – in the nomadic fashion of a technically temporary employee who roams the desert purposefully, and is handsomely compensated – from the Davis tent to a new "oasis" helmed by Crew Chief Mike Winters. Thirty-something full-timer Vic Carapazza also shifted from another crew to help Winters and No. 2 veteran holdover Mark Wegner complete the quartet; its season-opening composition of four guys – Winters, Wegner, Marty Foster and Mike Muchlinski – whose first names begin with the same letter, prompted one observer, an ex-umpire himself, to dub them as the "M-Squad." By late June, Torres had rejoined the Davis crew, as weekly moves in the Blue Chess Game continued to be made on the Big Board at 345 Park Avenue.

Carlos Torres, a native of Acarigua, set amid the oil-rich *Llanos* of Venezuela's northwestern Portuguesa state, along the east slope of the towering northern Andes, had begun his career as a U.S. professional umpire in the Rookie Gulf Coast League in 2009 at age 31. Even though he had moved to Florida, much of his family remained in Acarigua.

He tries to keep in touch by phone daily, comparing notes, with his best friend and the first Venezuela-born MLB umpire, Manny Gonzalez, who also resides in South Florida, as do several present and former *Blue Hombres*. Torres, a native of Barquisimeto in Lara state and only 15 months older than his countryman/colleague, most recently lived in the neighboring inland state of Portuguesa, about a 2½-hour drive from Gonzalez's hometown in coastal Carabobo state. Because of their similarities in native country, age, training and other factors, the two have almost identical plate "mechanics" – including consistent, measured game management and even in their strike-calling technique.

***

Also entering the 2016 season, another up-and-coming prospect, who has, at one time or another, been under the tutelage of Rich Garcia and Jorge Bauzá, was Ramon de Jesus, 32; he is a product of the Dominican Republic who was a highly regarded umpire in the Pacific Coast League (PCL) in the 2014 and 2015 seasons. De Jesus, though, began the 2016 campaign in the PCL as well, but made history on April 22, 2016, at Detroit's Comerica Park when he became the first umpire from his country to work a regular season major league game.

Filling in for full-time veteran Jim Wolf – older brother of recently retired longtime MLB pitcher Randy Wolf – de Jesus was assigned second base on a crew headed by Gary Cederstrom, who was conveniently right "next-door" at third base, readily accessible for between-innings advice. Eric Cooper was behind the plate, with Adrian Johnson at first base in a pitching duel between Cleveland's Josh Tomlin and Detroit's Justin Verlander, won by the Indians, 2-1.

Afterward, according to several sources who watched the contest in-person, de Jesus was calm and reflective as he responded to questions from designated "pool" reporters.

"It was a routine game, and that's what every umpire wants to have every night," de Jesus told the small reporting assemblage.

"He did a real good job," Crew Chief Cederstrom said. "I worked with him in spring training several times, and he's a very talented umpire."

"I became an umpire at the hand of Mónico Zayas, who in the Sports Ministry of Santo Domingo, gave me the opportunity to work in different amateur leagues, such as little leaguers up to the independent baseball league," de Jesus was quoted in early April 2016 from an interview with *Dominican Today*, which referred to him as Ramon de Jesus Ferrer, as he officially is known in his island homeland – the latter surname being his mother's maiden name. It is customary in Latin American countries to use the mother's birth name immediately following the paternal last name. In U.S. professional baseball records, the new Dominican pioneer is simply Ramon de Jesus.

After single Indians-Tigers games at Comerica on April 23 and 24 – the final date his MLB plate debut – instead of returning to the PCL, de Jesus hooked up in Denver, to call a Pittsburgh-Colorado series, with a Dale Scott-led crew that also featured Bob Davidson and Lance Barrett. De Jesus worked the plate in the third match-up of a scheduled four-game series, with the fourth meeting postponed because of cold weather and a rain-snow mix, but the Dominican remained with Scott's crew for at least two other series. (The make-up game was completed in Denver on June 9, officiated by Ted Barrett's crew, which included Will Little, Lance Barksdale and veteran *Blue Hombre* Angel Hernández – coming into the Colorado capital city a day early, since that group was scheduled to work the June 10-12 San Diego-Colorado series {Lance Barrett and Ted Barrett are not related.}.)

Those strange, small-world aspects that hover around professional sports – especially baseball – were fully in play by mid-May 2016. In a Cincinnati-at-Philadelphia series from May 13-15, de Jesus was a temporary replacement for Bill Welke on a crew comprised of John Hirschbeck, Latino umpire dean Garcia's longtime American League '90s sidekick; Carapazza, Garcia's son-in-law; and D.J. Reyburn, whom Garcia mentored closely in the years he was an umpire supervisor. In fact, Garcia conceded, with a smile, "Yeah, D.J. was one of my boys." Even though, in his lengthy career, Garcia had to "baby-sit" someone like Cuban *émigré* Armando Rodriguez, who resisted learning

English well, the Key West native found mentoring truly adult-behaving underlings such as Michigan's Reyburn and most Venezuelan aspirants to be a much more desirable and professional pursuit.

With Memorial Day 2016 nearing, the Dominican umpiring pioneer was impressive enough in his call-up to warrant hanging around in The Bigs longer. In a May 29 clash between two struggling AL clubs, Detroit and host Oakland, de Jesus did the plate in well under three hours on West's crew, as the Athletics prevailed, 4-2. The crew chief patrolled the bases with Kerwin Danley and Andy Fletcher.

Then, assigners were forced to accelerate that ongoing board game which goes into overdrive when a record number of umpire injuries, plus vacations and other approved absences, occur within a fairly narrow time window.

This meant that, just 21 hours and a two-hour flight up the Pacific Coast to Sea-Tac airport after the last pitch in Oakland, Fletcher was spelled by another regular West crew member, Mark Ripperger; the occasion was a four-game, home-and-home series – first at Seattle's Safeco Field on the Memorial holiday before finishing June 2 at San Diego's Petco Park, and de Jesus still as the crew's fourth – at least for the time being. In what more resembled a Chargers-Seahawks football battle, the Padres and Mariners combined for a whopping 79 runs in splitting the series. This also was momentous for the first arbiter from the eastern half of the island of Hispaniola being assigned as a call-up crew mate of baseball's longest-serving umpire – Ramon de Jesus rolling up an impressive and unforgettable roster of personal milestones, which also served as events significant in their historical and emotional magnitude to his *entire* little tropical country.

By June 18, the Cederstrom crew, also including Eric Cooper, Wolf, and de Jesus shifting back from West's quartet, reported for the opener of a three-game NL Central battle of the best-record-in-baseball Chicago Cubs versus the Pittsburgh Pirates at the Friendly Confines of Wrigley Field. It marked essentially the first chance for television viewers who did not have cable or satellite service to watch the Dominican umpire pacesetter in action; the game was seen largely by a national TV audience on the main Fox broadcast network, immediately following the third round of the U.S. Open golf tournament.

De Jesus lined up at second base, flanked by Cederstrom and Wolf at the corners, with Cooper behind home plate. In what continued to be a string of "firsts" for *Blue Hombre* Ramon de Jesus – from his April major league debut and seemingly almost weekly events – came two wrapped in one package, but not necessarily the kind one is anxious to open. The bundled deal comprised the initial instant replay/review of a de Jesus MLB call and his first overturned decision in the same instance.

It happened in the bottom of the fourth inning, as the Cubs' speedy Javier Baez took off from first base in an attempted steal. To the naked eye, at regular speed, it appeared not only that Pirates shortstop Jordy Mercer tagged out a sliding Baez, but re-applied a pair of follow-up tags – *somewhere* on the runner's uniform – when the Cub over-slid the bag at second. The rapid flurry of actions caused de Jesus to signal Baez "out." However, Baez encouraged his manager, Joe Maddon, to request a review. Then, with de Jesus standing next to him, Cederstrom got on the phone with replay review officials, who reversed the call. The Cubs went on to win, 4-3.

With that All-Star break beckoning, and de Jesus having bounced back to the Cederstrom crew – by then with Cooper, and Johnson back replacing Wolf – it made the call-up feel almost as if he were a first-time, mortgaged homeowner rather than a transient renter who resided in the attic and never unpacked his suitcase.

It is not totally certain whether Ramon de Jesus was in the group of Dominican umpires more than a decade earlier when MLB dispatched "ambassador" Rich Garcia to Santo Domingo to train the best prospects in the eastern Caribbean nation for potential work in U.S. professional leagues.

However, because de Jesus was a teen-ager already umpiring games during Garcia's foray, the "ambassador" said he believes the young man was indeed one of the Dominican prospects he trained with that Leatherneck touch.

Baseball academies, like those in the Dominican Republic and other countries, and funded by some big league teams, are increasingly popular; they serve as pre-U.S. umpire school instructional fonts – weeding out unpromising hopefuls and nurturing a blooming garden of possible future MLB umpires.

***

With time – and de Jesus's progress in giant steps – it seemed less likely he ever would come back to Triple-A. Yet, others continued either to await his PCL return or remain anxious for their own respective MLB call-up debuts. The lone call reversal notwithstanding, his colleagues may have had to wait a long time for de Jesus's "homecoming," considering his otherwise overall high marks

Among those assigned to the PCL or co-equal AAA International League (IL) included Chris Gonzalez, Albert Ruiz, Roberto Ortiz, Alex Ortiz and Robert Moreno. The Ortizes are not related, nor is American Chris Gonzalez related to Venezuelan MLB umpire Manny Gonzalez. All of the listed were likely to have been major league call-ups sometime in 2016.

***

Then there was the fireworks-like ascension over the past several years of Angel Campos and Ramon Armendariz; but the fiery rise fizzled out like a burnt sparkler on the Fourth of July. The talented, likeable pair, only a year apart in age and who grew up 40 miles from each other at different ends of the sprawling Los Angeles Basin, both began the trek toward achieving the MLB pinnacle at age 22.

Campos has been a battler ever since his birth on Sept. 22, 1973, in Montclair, Calif., an older suburb with a 73 percent Latino population, straddling the Los Angeles/San Bernardino county line, roughly midway between the respective county seats of the same names.

At 5-9, while not the littlest guy, he was smaller than many of his teammates when he competed in various sports at Montclair High School, and certainly shorter than the average major league umpire during his MLB career from 2007 to 2014.

"He was an up-and-down guy," Jorge Bauzá said of Campos, who once was one of the latter's prize pupils. Up-and-down, in this case, is "inside baseball" terminology for a Triple-A operative competent enough to be called up frequently to the majors temporarily before being sent back down until the next call-up opening. Outside of injuries or serious illnesses, the main reason for most call-ups is the three or four weeks' paid vacation taken by the regulars – typically in mid- to late summer, before the heat of fall pennant races and after the early season hubbub. Some MLB umpires, who have an inkling they might be working the annual All-Star Game in mid-July, have been known to wrap earned vacation days around that date – leaving potential added call-up opportunities for the Triple-A umpire crowd.

Bauzá, Puerto Rican by birth but a longtime South Floridian, is a former veteran minor league umpire who is Field Evaluator and Instructor of Umpire Development for Minor League Baseball (MiLB); his manifold duties include traveling often during the offseason to Latin America and the Caribbean to recruit and develop potential professional baseball officials, and also is a key instructor at the MiLB Umpire Academy, on the site of the old Dodgertown at Vero Beach, Fla.

Bauzá's state-of-the-art version of an old-time Rolodex® is the gigantic database in the laptop he carries with him everywhere, containing information more valuable, it seems, than the Dead Sea Scrolls themselves. Inside the little computer are names, phone numbers and/or email addresses of virtually *everyone in* the minor leagues, as well as each prospect with whom he has had, or will have, contact.

***

It might be considered almost a medical miracle that Angel Campos lasted beyond the 2010 season after an appendicitis attack during a rain delay before the start of a Sept. 11, 2010, night game at Cleveland's lakeside Progressive Field between the hometown Indians and Minnesota Twins, and resultant emergency appendectomy at a local hospital. The ruptured appendix ended his season. The organ is known to possess no specific bodily function, according to medical website *WebMD.com*, yet conversely, a rupture can prove potentially fatal.

However, Campos, demonstrating a strong will to live, weathered that storm. He returned to his on-field trade during spring training in 2011 and proceeded to split time between The Bigs and the Triple-A PCL until the end of the 2014 season, when he was released just after his 42nd birthday. All told, he had completed 473 MLB games, 111 behind the plate. Despite the slight setback at this stage, though, Campos harbored hopes of working his way back into permanency in The Show.

During his career of almost eight full seasons at baseball's highest level, he enjoyed his share of memorable highlights – although officials in any professional sport, to be universally accepted, and respected, must go quietly about their business almost as if they were the equivalent of *ghosts*. In other words, do your job, but do not outwardly call attention to yourself; let players, managers and coaches do that.

Just the same as he desired if injured by a hard-hit ball, a guy like Campos, who wore No. 84, had no intention of calling attention to *himself* when felled by the appendicitis attack. Better yet that it happened *during a rain delay*, he told himself, as the contest wound up going 12 innings, with the Indians winning, 1-0.

When such an unfortunate and inopportune event occurs, a regular four-man umpiring crew is reduced by one – meaning the Californian's three partners worked the entire game, with Crew Chief Brian Gorman stationed behind the plate, but the remaining pair of base umpires, Paul Nauert and Tony Randazzo, having to hustle an "extra notch," as Chef Emeril would say, to cover the trio of "bags."

(If an umpire is around long enough, working an average of 140 games a season, he personally sees some injury or misfortune – affecting himself or a crew member – that etch another entry into his psyché. So it is with Brian Gorman. As documented in an earlier chapter, he also would be crew chief when plate partner Manny Gonzalez got knocked out of service for almost a month after a foul ball injured him during a Colorado Rockies-New York Mets game at Citi Field during the 2013 season. Gorman's father, Tom, who passed away in 1986, was a National League umpire for 25 years from the 1950s to the '70s, then signed on as an umpire supervisor. To honor his father's memory, Brian Gorman, who became a National League arbiter in 1991, wears No. 9, same as Tom. Other than the Crawfords, Gormans, Hirschbecks, Runges, Welkes and Wendelstedts, the only bloodlines in history to have provided multiple big league umpires comprised the late father, Lou DiMuro, and his son, Mike. Lou, who was an AL umpire for 19 years, died in 1982 when run over by a car while out walking; Mike is in his 18th season calling balls and strikes in the "penthouse," and adheres to the numbers tradition by wearing dad's old "16.")

All regular MLB umpires are subject to a game-to-game rotation whereby, at season's end, each crew member has worked roughly 25 percent of every start at each of the three bases or the plate.

Although no umpire in his right mind ever would admit publicly he prefers one position over the others, Angel Campos probably harbors a secret desire toward being at second base. Why? Because he was at that spot over the years during games when the most positive historical happenings of his career took place.

The first of those memorable moments was the San Francisco Giants' Puerto Rican southpaw Jonathan Sanchez's no-hitter on July 10, 2009, against the visiting NL West rival San Diego Padres at AT&T Park.

Even better was to be an up-close, first-hand witness to the perfect game spun in the same "yard" on June 13, 2012, by another Giants pitcher – this time, right-hander Matt Cain, in an 8-0 win over the Houston Astros. (The last previous time a San Francisco pitcher had no-hit Houston, then the expansion Colt .45s, who later became the Astros, was by future Hall of Fame, high-leg-kicking right-hander and Dominican Republic native Juan Marichal on June 15, 1962, at since-demolished Candlestick Park, just five bayside miles south of AT&T.)

***

Getting back to the post-MLB relationship between Angel Campos and Jorge Bauzá, who seemingly is everyone's best friend in the minor leagues and the entire realm of U.S. umpire development activities, the connection never has been severed.

Consequently, it is no surprise someone in his position stays in touch even with those who have not been under his *aegis* for some time, including Campos.

"He called me (in 2015) to ask me about doing international games," such as those as distant as Taiwan and Australia, among others, Bauzá said.

Especially in the Land Down Under – like much of South America, situated in the Southern Hemisphere, where our winter is their summer – December through February means a lot of baseball below the Equator. Hence, a crying need for umpires, like Campos, who bear a solid MLB pedigree.

With the World Baseball Softball Confederation (WBSC) actively seeking eager, experienced arbiters to call games, endless opportunities abound for those willing to be paid and live abroad, despite sometimes thorny language issues.

If you believe transcending cultural and linguistic barriers is not possible in the wake of seeing the MLB "Dream Bubble" burst, consult Ramon Armendariz. He had to start anew with the special set of skills he will carry with him forever – wherever there are baseball diamonds.

***

Having achieved part-time status for a short period as a major league umpire following his experience in the ultra-competitive Venezuelan winter leagues and as a game-caller in the AAA Pacific Coast League, Ramon Armendariz found that umpiring in the island nation of Taiwan (aka Chinese Taipei, Free China and Nationalist China), while posing certain unique challenges, was not difficult. After all, he enjoyed an advantage over virtually any Taiwanese colleague, carrying in his "back pocket" that evidence of the taste of the Holy Water he had ingested from the U.S. big leagues, worldwide baseball's most adored shrine.

Most recently junior varsity baseball coach for the Santa Monica High School ("Samohi," more familiarly) Vikings who retains his umpiring expertise by calling college games in the Western Athletic Conference and PAC-12, like the *real* Norsemen of yore, Armendariz always has had an adventurous streak.

The desire to make, not just lemonade, but a lemon-flavored *mojito*, out of a basket of the tart, yellow citrus fruit figuratively left on his porch in 2007, triggered his wanderlust. Armendariz wound up in Taiwan, calling balls and strikes in the Chinese Professional Baseball League, in the wake of his release from Major League Baseball when the '07 season ended. His MLB experience, all strictly as a call-up to fill in for the permanent umpiring staff during vacations or other approved absences, consisted of just over five-dozen regular-season games from '04 to '07.

Similar to Campos officiating a no-hitter and perfecto, maybe the zenith for Los Angeles-born Armendariz, manning first base, was July 27, 2004, when future Hall of Fame right-hander Greg Maddux, still with the Chicago Cubs then, got his 299th career win over the host Milwaukee Brewers in a day game at Miller Park.

The 1995 graduate of MLB/MiLB-approved Wendelstedt Umpire School found his two-season sojourn in the Chinese-speaking island country to be rewarding and truly educational. Yet he yearned to fulfill the now-impossible dream of returning to The Show. When, in the offseason as a then-current MLB fill-in, the lifelong Angeleno was invited to call games in the 2006 World Baseball Classic, run by the WBSC, he never envisioned he would be umpiring on the other side of the Pacific Rim two years later.

***

Minor league levels assigned to the rest of the Latino umpires when the 2016 regular season began were (designations tentative, subject to change during season):

- **Class AA:** Roberto Teran, Charlie Ramos, David Arrieta Quintero, Nestor Ceja;
- **High-A:** Adrian Gonzalez, Derek Gonzales, Edwin Moscoso, Jonathan Parra-Valencia, Jesse Orozco;
- **Class A:** Alexis Trujillo, Ricardo Estrada, Luis Hernandez, David Martinez, Anthony Perez, Jose Matamoros, JC Velez-Morales, José Navas Corzo, Jesus Gonzalez;
- **Short Season-A:** Emil Jiménez Pernalete, Raúl Moreno Benitez.

***

Counting every domestic league from the AL and NL, down through Class A, Rookie and Instructional levels, when the 2016 season began in April, there was an estimated active total of 33 *Blue Hombres*, or Latino umpires, from either the United States, Puerto Rico or four other countries, employed by U.S. pro organizations.

9

VINCE DELGADO
IT 'REALLY' WENT TO HIS HEAD

When Vince Delgado still was playing baseball in Orange County, Calif., back in the 1970s and '80s – at every level from Little League (LL), to Senior LL, El Modena High and Santa Ana College – his coaches constantly reminded their athletes: "Keep your head in the ball game."

Vincent Delgado, back then more widely known as "Vinny," rather than the more grown-up "Vince," always complied – dutiful sort he has been throughout life. Delgado was so intent on the heads-up advice, by the time he evolved into being a promising minor league umpire in the late '80s, he was already on an accelerated career path as a *Blue Hombre*; the 5-foot-10, 190-pounder was diving headlong into a vortex that more than likely would exit by dumping him someday onto a major league field of dreams.

He *did* indeed wind up working in a big league ballpark, but the exact details will be disclosed later in this chapter.

Everywhere he went, starting as a high-schooler in the El Modena section of the City of Orange, he was bitten by the umpiring bug. Delgado possessed the basic natural talent, instincts and other requisite ingredients to be an exceptional on-field arbiter. That was indisputable, yet he also had the constant good fortune at every juncture along the way somehow to be in front of key people who had interest in – and power to act – enabling him to advance rapidly up each succeeding step. However, as just promised, more on that in a moment.

More recently, Delgado, 52, when interviewed exclusively for this book in March and May 2016, has worn a different shade of blue uniform as a veteran law enforcement officer in Orange County. Specifically, Inspector Vincent Delgado is a highly respected and sought-after polygraph examiner with the Anaheim Police Department, his full-time employer the past two decades.

In conjunction with that profession, he also spends many hours during the Major League Baseball (MLB) regular season between April and October – at home games of Latino owner Arte Moreno's Los Angeles Angels of Anaheim at Angel Stadium of Anaheim. His "moonlighting" role as a Resident Security Agent, officially an MLB employee, is in addition to the police polygraph job.

"It's my eighth season," Delgado said regarding the 2016 campaign that was about to begin less than a month after his first of multiple interviews for *Blue Hombres*. "There are 70 of us, nationwide, and, yes, in Toronto, too." The security agents, stationed in each of the 30 MLB stadiums, offer an extra layer of plainclothes comfort to spectators and game participants alike in this age of unpredictable terrorist attacks or other unforeseen events.

The hybrid polygraph expert/ballpark security agent was there, merely as a spectator, at the same site where, a decade later, he would be working his MLB gig. It was in then-Anaheim Stadium – or more familiarly, The Big A; Delgado perhaps was thinking back, wishing he was part of the on-field officiating crew, at a momentous occasion for his good friend, Alfonso "Fonzy" Marquez, who lived at the time in neighboring Fullerton. That was in April 1997 during an exhibition game. It was the first time Marquez had worked at the big league level.

(*"Hey, dude! You promised us you'd get back to this guy's umpire story. What gives?"* The little wag gnome, who appears occasionally to exhort the author, has now forced the author to comply with the request.)

***

Vince Delgado's umpire saga was filled with hope, the talent to turn wishful thinking into concrete accomplishments, and a burning desire to weld those factors – using life's soldering iron, so to speak – into a harmonious blend of career-advancing activities that had him destined for the majors someday.

However, July 23, 1989, marked the end of what had been a constantly upward spiral in the professional umpiring ranks for Vincent M. Delgado. After his first season in the rookie-tier Pioneer League in several Rocky Mountain and Pacific Northwest states, plus all or parts of three seasons – from 1986-88 – in the Advanced-A California League, he was working in a two-man system with regular partner Joe Yonto in the Midwest League (MWL). The MWL, although also a Class A circuit, had 14 teams in two divisions and was considered a step up from the older, nine-team Cal League. With many aging ballparks scattered mostly in old river towns in four states – Illinois, Indiana, Iowa and Wisconsin – there were a lot of "short porches" in the outfield, making inviting home-run targets. (Among aspiring prospects with Delgado and Yonto in the 1989 Midwest League were current MLB veteran umpires Marty Foster and Paul Nauert. Foster, who grew up in Colorado but now resides in Wisconsin, hails from an umpiring family; an older cousin, now-retired Joe Rossi – to whom Foster always referred as "Uncle Joe" – was a longtime college and prep umpire who until recently hosted an annual umpire benefit dinner and golf tournament in Colorado.)

The result of the friendly fences was, statistically, the MWL led all U.S. minor leagues in home runs, but also in strikeouts – indicating a dinger-or-whiff atmosphere among Midwest batters, with comparatively fewer singles, doubles or triples. It was in this little world that Delgado and Yonto existed in the '89 season. As best as the story can be recollected – amid pounding headaches and occasional "fuzzy-eyed" horizons multiplied by past serious concussions suffered by one of the duo – they drove together every three nights, on average, in Delgado's used Nissan pickup truck. A typical, roundabout trip could go from, say, from Beloit to Peoria to South Bend to Cedar Rapids and back to where they had started in Wisconsin, all in two weeks' time. Their employer, Minor League Baseball (MiLB), paid each roughly $2,000 in monthly salary, and $45 *per diem* money to cover food and lodging, which usually meant any one of many, 30-buck-a-night "Patel motels," like that depicted in the Denzel Washington movie *Mississippi Masala*, where the aroma of curry wafted in the small lobbies as they registered for their multi-night stays. The pair also was reimbursed for gas mileage at a rate, set by the Internal Revenue Service, of 29 cents a mile.

That steamy, June evening in Yonto's hometown of South Bend, Ind., less than three miles south of the giant shadow cast by Notre Dame's "Touchdown Jesus," marked the biggest turning point in 25-year-old Vince Delgado's life. He and his umpiring partner, after driving half the previous night into the northern Indiana city of Yonto's birth from a three-game series in Peoria, Ill., bedded down at the home of the local product's parents. Then, following a late, wake-up brunch prepared by the latter's mother, the two MWL umpires made their way to "The Cove," site of the opener in a three-game set pitting the South Bend White Sox against the visiting Appleton (Wis.) Foxes in a battle of two teams in the middle of the standings. The stadium's nickname was derived from the local baseball hero for which the structure – then only two years old – was named, Stanley Coveleskie; it did resemble most of the other Midwest playing sites, being power-hitter-friendly, with symmetrical dimensions of 336 feet down both foul lines and only 406 to dead-center field.

Remember that, while the Midwest was a league where hitters often launched the long ball when making contact, hard shots were supposed to leave the yard, not hit umpires. However, in the top of third inning, a foul ball off an Appleton bat ricocheted and did exactly what Delgado did not want – it knocked his steel-and-rubber-padded face mask so hard that the mask flew off, and the plate umpire reeled to the ground. After a delay and a few minutes of attention from the White Sox medical and training staff, Delgado wound up finishing the game, but with what felt like a timpani-laced migraine headache – a precursor to a concert of percussion drums that would beat regularly inside his skull for years thereafter.

Following the game, supposedly the mental re-run depicted visions of Yonto – son of a late Fighting Irish football playing and coaching legend also named Joe Yonto, and himself a head baseball coach at a small Catholic college south of South Bend since 2006 – driving Delgado, in the latter's pickup, to a local emergency room, where an examination revealed a pre-diagnosis of a serious concussion. With MWL headquarters minutes away in downtown South Bend and Delgado advised to spend the next night in hospital for further observation, Yonto went personally to the league office to relay the unfortunate news and to ensure quickly he would have a last-minute replacement partner for that evening's game … and, basically, it turned out, forever.

That assignment in South Bend was the final time Vince Delgado would umpire a baseball game. That "bug," which originally had bitten him years ago, suddenly had transformed from an itch into a severe headache.

"Naturally, I was devastated," the Californian admitted. "But, you know, I guess I saw this coming after the Cal League. I probably fooled myself, thinking it never would happen again."

Translation: The South Bend concussion was not the first for Delgado; he had suffered similar injuries during his second season in the California League in 1987 when deflected balls from bats twice hit him flush on the front of his mask, hard enough in both previous cases to bend the steel bars.

***

Before too long, Vincent Delgado embarked on his law enforcement career, perhaps reasoning that, leaving one job involuntarily where rules were observed almost religiously, it made sense to start anew in another which followed similar strictures. In both instances, those who opted for either of the two professions had "keeping the peace" as a central tenet.

Progressing up the ladder at the Anaheim Police Department, Delgado earned the title of Investigator, and absorbed every tidbit and detail about polygraph examinations as he could – winding up as a regionally and nationally recognized "go to" guy when other police agencies needed his services. He did not have to tell people he could play a game of Truth or Dare; he was living a *truly* righteous existence in ferreting out felonious fibbers.

Delgado's longtime friend, Rich Garcia, was an American League (AL) crew chief at the same time the Anaheim-cop-to-be was coming up through the minors. They both were instructors each January at Joe Brinkman's Florida umpire school. The two renewed the friendship in 2009, when Garcia still was an MLB umpire supervisor and Delgado entered his first season in MLB security at The Big A.

Garcia, a traditionalist who believes fans, players, managers/coaches, umpires and other employees have a right to be safe and have an enjoyable experience at the ballpark, said that, since Delgado was unable to fulfill his original umpiring dream, he is happy to see him and his colleagues in well-deserved resident security roles.

***

"I started umpiring my junior year of high school to make extra money," said Vince Delgado, who also played baseball for the El Modena Vanguards in high school and first base in junior college in nearby Santa Ana. "Matt Ward, my high school teammate, encouraged me to be an umpire.

"My first game, I got noticed, right off the bat. I did the plate and wasn't nervous at all. I didn't know what I was doing," but he nevertheless drew special attention. "One of the Little League district umpire guys saw me, and, while I was a senior in high school, the Villa Park Little League hired me as a permanent umpire. It was a good deal; I got paid $20 a game and did three games a week … and I still was in high school," he added, an almost-suspended air of disbelief in his voice.

Every time Delgado advanced to a slightly higher level – through Senior Little League, high schools and college games of smaller Southern California schools that belonged to the National Association of Intercollegiate Athletics (NAIA) – somehow, some way, there would be *somebody* in the stands who would throw him feelers to move up one more notch. One such baseball-savvy person dared suggest he consider enrolling in one of several umpire schools in Florida, where those who successfully completed the month-long courses each January were almost automatically offered minor league contracts as soon as they doffed their graduation caps and gowns.

Trouble was, tuition kept rising annually and was approaching $4,000 (including only one daily meal covered), so in 1985, at age 21, Delgado, who was good at saving money, combined those funds with gifts and loans from family and friends. The school he selected was operated by then-still-active AL umpire Brinkman. A suave operator with a full head of typical '80s-style, permed, salt-and-pepper hair and a neatly trimmed mustache, Brinkman was capable of playing good-cop/bad-cop with his students all by himself;

moments after berating an errant, would-be arbiter with "constructive criticism," Brinkman would launch into one of his "shithouse tapes" umpire tell-all stories – many based on first-hand incidences – that would have the group rolling in classroom aisles with laughter.

"I didn't really know what to make of him from one day to the next. I chose his school over the others because I had been impressed by him at umpire clinics," Delgado said.

Upon graduation, the current polygraph expert proceeded to instructional-league assignments in his initial taste of professional game-calling in 1985. He then moved to the short-season, rookie-level Pioneer League in 1986, followed by two seasons-plus (covering the rest of '86 and '87-'88) – and two head injuries – in the California League, and his officiating fate being sealed at South Bend in 1989. During Delgado's tenure as a West Coast minor league umpire, the Cal circuit included clubs in San Bernardino, Riverside, Palm Springs, Bakersfield, Fresno, Visalia, Salinas, San Jose, Modesto, Stockton and Reno, Nev.

***

In August 1987, Delgado caught up with old partner, Coloradan Ken Franek, 72 games after the first of what would be three concussions suffered by Delgado, spread out over a year's calendar time but reaching from one season to the next. In retrospect today, however, Delgado often must ponder with nagging doubt: *"Was I ever really 'well enough' to come back?"*

It was at the Cal League's one non-California stop in "The Biggest Little City in the World," where, instead of Delgado hitting a jackpot, it felt as if *he* had been hit by a giant, slow-cooking pot. What a crock! And this time, at Reno's Moana Stadium, the host Padres were facing a team, the Modesto A's, that, it turned out, seemed to be following Delgado and Franek like a proverbial black cat. The playing site, which was demolished in 2012 to make way for a more modern stadium, bore a small arch at one entrance which fittingly stated: "Biggest Little Ballpark in the World."

The rangy (6-3, 215 pounds) Franek, son of a Colorado State Patrol officer whose duty area was a multi-county chunk of the sparsely populated

Eastern Plains, had been a three-sport athlete at Colorado State University-Pueblo (then known as the University of Southern Colorado).

The Delgado-Franek duo must have reckoned there were worse places for a young, two-man umpiring crew to be "beating the bushes" than low-humidity Reno on a late-summer night like this one in 1987. However, the SoCal half of this pairing likely might want to take back those thoughts, after the life-altering events that happened.

Delgado's constant on-field *alter ego*/traveling partner gets a painful look on his face trying to recall verbally the fateful game in Reno when his brother-in-arms went down for the count; Delgado might as well have been the unwitting challenger knocked permanently to the canvas by a boxing champion. That is how hard it is when a baseball tipped off a bat zooms directly into the mask's steel veneer – at speeds often well exceeding 100 miles an hour, requiring a nanosecond to "travel" mere inches.

Admitted Franek: "I didn't know the seriousness of what transpired" – which had its genesis months before in Bakersfield, the Los Angeles Dodgers' similarly named Class A farm club; the little Dodgers had resumed their blood-sport rivalry with the visiting Fresno Giants, the San Joaquin Valley spawns of *their* big league parents, the San Francisco Giants. Trouble was, while umpires were supposed to be somewhat exempt from "donating plasma samples," that bubble of immunity unfortunately did not extend to Vince Delgado.

In the series at Bakersfield – which mirrored one between the arch-rival squads in Fresno the previous month – it was the turn of Delgado, two years senior and an *ad hoc* mentor to Franek, to work the plate in the series opener. In the third inning, figurative lightning struck, representing what in every way seemed an ominous signal of Delgado's fate – a future which was seriously tested later in Reno, of course, and, ultimately sealed the following year in the MWL.

Hence, the beginning of the eventual end of the promising umpiring path for Vincent Delgado was clearly at hand. The games in Bakersfield and Reno were bound by the same, simple action – that of a sharply hit foul ball tipping off a wood bat and going directly to Delgado's supposedly protective mask, for which the black steel was reinforced by the beige deerskin padding covering the chin and forehead.

"I remember the first time, specifically, because of where I was hit, my positioning, everything. I guess the stars aligned," concussive pain still radiating externally as he graphically described the impact almost three decades later. The ball hit the bottom part of the mask, where a small steel loop extended less than an inch, just below the deerskin "cushion," to protect, presumably, the Adam's apple. "It bent up the mask considerably. The Fresno trainer, who later moved to the major leagues, came out, and I spit up some blood like from a tongue bite, stopping it with water he gave me," Delgado said.

"I heard a 'thud' and watched Vinny immediately go down," Franek said, adding that he, too, was devastated, being the main, up-close witness to the downhill slide of a potential major league officiating career.

As for Delgado, despite having morphed into a fuzzy mental state, he somehow was able to complete the game at Sam Lynn Ballpark, a remodeled relic dating back to the league's birth at the onset of World War II. Yet, he admitted, "I don't remember finishing the game. I remember the next night; I did the bases and felt terrible." He had been taken to the hospital after the initial game, undergone observation, was treated and released – a misleading mental seed planted in his aching head, indicating he was ready to work the next game with his trusted sidekick. It was clear, otherwise, that he was ill-prepared even to do the bases.

After Delgado had to return to the clubhouse in the second inning when a baseball hit him in the shoulder, one of the Fresno team's staffers drove him back to the hospital, where the young umpire was diagnosed with multiple injuries – the more serious one being the severe concussion. There was an aggravated sense of pain, as the combined force of the face shot and more recent shoulder injury caused his head to feel like giant bass drum being pounded upon with an extra-large mallet.

"It did happen early in the game. ... I had to go into the dressing room in the third inning and put on the plate gear, and finished the game basically by myself," added Franek, who – in a somewhat bizarre sort of a way – actually *did* have a bit of accompaniment the final two innings. Moreover, what ensued until game's end gave him a taste of exactly how minor league umpiring would be for the next 72 contests without his wounded partner – or until their fateful reunion in Reno.

Covering the game for a local broadcast station was a reporter who had attended umpire school.

"He went in and used Vinny's uniform, and came out in like the top of the eighth inning to *help* me finish the game," said Franek, spiking the bittersweet remembrance with an understandable shot of sarcasm, chased by an added drop of disgust. "I should've finished the game myself," because he said the reporter who became a self-appointed "vigilante" umpire mechanically mishandled a play that caused an argument in the bottom of the eighth.

"With no runners on base, the batter hit a low, soft fly ball toward the right-fielder," Franek continued. Based on his precise recollection in describing how the play unfolded, it was clear, in retrospect, to anyone who ever has umpired in a two-man system, that the reporter-turned-temporary arbiter erred in judgment and application as the play went into motion. "He ran into the infield," just beyond the bag, "which the base umpire needs to do, to determine if he should go out to right field on the play for a possible trap/shoestring catch or come into the infield and pivot to watch the batter-runner touch first while always also keeping aware of the ball's exact location.

"If the base umpire comes into the infield, then the call is the home plate umpire's call. So, seeing the reporter/umpire coming into the infield, I determined that the play for the trap/shoestring play was a catch," Franek said.

Thus, by precisely re-creating an instant "snapshot" of this first-hand scenario for this book, the plate umpire has graphically illustrated the incorrect way the fill-in umpire had unwittingly drawn the ire of the home team's manager. That manager, Kevin Kennedy, would go on to become skipper of two American League teams – the Texas Rangers and Boston Red Sox – between 1993 and 1996. Kennedy later progressed to win an Emmy Award as a Fox Sports baseball analyst, and has been doing L.A. Dodgers' radio work since 2014.

Correct hand signals being critical in determining such basic options as "safe/out" or "catch/no catch," then conveying them quickly and clearly to anyone involved in the game, were not used by the "reporter/umpire" who had *glommed* on to Franek's orbit, with minimal consent at best, only to spoil the occasion further with poor mechanics.

"The problem the reporter/umpire had, as he was running, he signaled the 'safe' mechanic, which *also* means 'no catch'," Franek explained. "That's when the Dodgers' manager, Kevin Kennedy, came running out to me, ready to argue my call of a catch. He wanted me to defer my call to the reporter/base umpire, because it was opposite of my call.

"Kevin would not relinquish his debate, so he ended up getting ejected from the game. Kevin did not realize this flaw in the two-man system. But it is one of many, I told him over and over again, when the base umpire comes into the infield, it is my call and my call stands," said the Colorado resident, who has maintained a trim, muscular physique to enable him to officiate football and basketball.

"Kevin earned the big 'heave-ho,' by one simple mistake; I told him, after I let him have his say-so, 'I am going back to my position (which was behind the plate); if you follow me, or you're still standing here, you're done'!"

Kennedy then took only two steps with Franek, who, just as quickly, kept his word, and showed the manager the quickest route to the showers at old Sam Lynn, which opened on Bakersfield's North Side, along the Kern River, in 1941, and was renovated in 1993-4; it is one of only two baseball venues in organized professional baseball – the other Wahconah Park in Pittsfield, Mass. – where batters face directly west. Sam Lynn, reputable baseball historians agree, also boasts organized baseball's shortest distance to dead-center-field at a measly 354 feet from home plate. Maybe that was a concession to batters for the designers' original mistake of the west-facing hitting scheme.

Arch-rival Fresno, slightly larger and about a two-hour drive north on the 99 Freeway – occasionally reduced to "no-visibility" conditions when "Tule fog" or peat dust from the millions of acres of rich farmland envelop the road – has progressed even more on ball diamonds. The city's aging, longtime ballfield, John Euless Park, still sits astride its football/soccer "bedfellow," Ratcliffe Stadium, in a park belonging to nearby Fresno City College. With Fresno today still a Giants' farm club, but in the top-drawer Triple-A Pacific Coast League as the Grizzlies, the newer baseball venue is named Chukchansi Park, for the Native American-owned resort/casino that paid $16 million for naming rights to Grizzlies Stadium, which was completed in 2002.

***

Once back home in Orange County to rehabilitate during his 72-day hiatus, Vince Delgado received what one could only term the latter portion of "cradle-to-concussion" coverage. He immediately called his primary care physician who also was a sports medicine specialist and famed longtime California Angels' and former Los Angeles Rams' team doctor. That PCP, Dr. Jules Razinski, had delivered Vincent M. Delgado into the world in an Anaheim hospital in 1964. Consequently, the sidelined, 25-year-old umpire, instead of having his umbilical cord severed, a quarter-century later, was having his uppermost pain being treated by the same doctor.

Other than some tests and necessary extra-strength painkillers, the primary rehab, Delgado said, consisted mainly of "just doing nothing but rest" until he felt well enough for a return to Cal League diamonds. His tenure in the league ended, of course, with the second concussion, in Reno, two weeks after his "comeback."

While the cop-in-waiting was sidelined, his partner, the son-of-a-cop, logged 72 consecutive "dish" starts in Cal League games, working with college-level replacement umpires – most of whom had "stage fright" and declined when offered the home plate assignment.

Amid their collective imagined "fears" must have lurked a contrary, underlying realization that, when you're behind the plate, you:

- Are in better control of the game;
- Have much better physical protection with added equipment;
- Are facing the field of play most of time without needing to make many awkward sideways or backwards movements or turns;

148

- Get to keep track, in conjunction/coordination with the official scorekeeper, of the game's every aspect, on your little-bitty writing pad – provided you didn't leave your pen at home or in the car;
- Are perceived as "boss," being umpire-in-chief, even though you and your base partner are technically equal in game administration and each of you is the other's "best friend" during a game.

***

As he had done after completing Brinkman's school in January 1985, the future polygraph examiner returned each winter to Florida as an instructor at that academy. That included his "rehab" off-seasons of 1987-88 and 1988-89, between California and Midwest league game-calling.

***

Looking back to well before he had reported for his Midwest assignment, Vince Delgado formed a lasting bond with an African-American former All-America outfielder, and college teammate of late Hall-of-Famer Tony Gwynn, out of L.A.'s Dorsey High and San Diego State University who today is a longtime respected MLB umpire. Kerwin Danley, renowned for his ubiquitous freckles and infectious, gap-toothed smile, and Delgado clicked immediately with each other; just as it had been with Franek, they became lifelong best friends traveling the Cal League in 1986.

Of the numerous games the two collaborated on, one sticks out in Delgado's mind. The site was San Jose's venerable Municipal Stadium, home of the Bees, an Advanced-A club and the only one in the nine-team league without a major league affiliation. Therefore, the Bees – the closest thing to an "independent" in an otherwise-affiliated league – became a sort of Betty Ford Clinic of baseball. The San Jose organization willingly signed one-time big league stars – many of them substance-abusers still young enough to play well, when clean and sober; or 40-something "wash-ups" attempting to regain glory they perhaps never had – to single-year contracts. The most notable, yet also most tragic, was the late southpaw reliever Steve Howe, who was a No. 1 draft choice of the Dodgers in 1980 and eventually died at age 48 in 2006 when his truck rolled over; post-mortem toxicology tests revealed evidence of methamphetamine in Howe's blood.

This was the aura in 1986 when the Bees were at home to face the Modesto A's in a "night" contest that began in gradually dimming sunlight shining on most of the field.

With Delgado behind the plate, and Danley stationed down the line beyond the bag at first base, one out and the bases empty, and the visitors batting in an early inning, Félix José, a future journeyman utility player in both U.S. and Japan major leagues, was batting. With daylight still present, he tapped a roller toward shortstop, and hustled down the line to first, with Delgado trailing right behind him to ensure the player stayed in the "running lane" approaching the base. The play at first was not close – in UmpireSpeak, "wide open" – so Danley, who was responsible for the decision, indicated "out" from the spot in the infield a few feet from the bag to which he always would hustle, pivot to make the call while completely stopped in a squared-up stance.

José, instead of turning to go back to the dugout, inexplicably raced toward Danley, punching him in the chest, as A's Manager Tommie Reynolds sped to the scene to "rescue" José, who Danley had automatically ejected, once the player touched him.

"I was pretty new in professional baseball, but in doing colleges, high schools and various youth leagues for years, I still had never seen anything exactly like that – before or since," Delgado said. Danley told him he was worried the often-unpredictable league president would fine or suspend him, despite the one half of the Double-D crew not having done a thing to precipitate or provoke José's actions.

***

It certainly was quite appropriate that Golden State native Vince Delgado spent more than half his professional umpiring career in the California League. After all, one of the "infants" in the West Coast circuit's first year, 1941, was the Anaheim Aces, who played home games in busy La Palma Park. Delgado was born two miles away at Martin Luther Hospital in 1964 – long after the Aces had been "flushed" from the league's deck, and two years following the Angels' arrival.

His ancestors had migrated to the Los Angeles/Orange County area from Mexico's Pacific Coast states of Jalisco and Sinaloa a couple of generations before his birth.

***

Considering all those coaching admonitions such as "keep your *head* in the ball game," "use your *head*" and others, Inspector Delgado now does not even bat an eyelash when, as an MLB Resident Security Agent at The Big A, he hears cautionary sayings related to the eye – all the while remaining "heads-up."

10
JORGE BAUZÁ
THE MAN WHO WEARS MANY HATS

Feeling glad, even blessed, on this sunny Thursday morning inside the concourse of Simon Bolívar International Airport, *21 kilometros* (13 miles) from the heart of Venezuela's bustling capital city, Caracas, a 40-something man, toting a plaid, vinyl traveling bag, pauses no more than 10 seconds, glancing quickly at his waterproof Tag Heuer wristwatch.

Without even a second's more hesitation, he takes off running, the long, pliable bag hooked to his right forefinger and slung back over the same-side shoulder – Immediate Destination: Gate 41; Ultimate Destination: Las Américas International Airport, just outside Santo Domingo, the Caracas capital counterpart in the Dominican Republic.

He has barely 18 minutes before the Aserca Airlines MD-87, an American-made jet, built by McDonnell Douglas Corp., is scheduled to take off. Once the one-hour, 40-minute non-stop flight is airborne and zipping north across the middle of the Caribbean Sea with this hurried, but not harried, soul aboard, he can at least relax for an hour or so before opening the laptop to check his Dominican itinerary. To get out above totally open water, the jet's route is squeezed between the string-of-pearls islands that spell the transition from Netherlands Antilles to Lesser Antilles on the right, and the three larger, ABC Islands – Aruba, Bonaire and Curaçao – in the distance beyond the port side.

So who is this guy traveling lightly and moving briskly? And why is he so "glad"?

Easy answers. His name: Jorge Bauzá. Knowing he always schedules his time from Point A to Point B to Point C in tight intervals, rather than wearing dressy leather loafers, he is *glad* to have opted for a pair of comfy tennis shoes – the best choice for the sudden point-to-point dashes. Bauzá also is aboard his favorite non-U.S. carrier, Aserca, which he otherwise uses in Venezuela to do quick "hops" from city to city *within* the baseball-loving country; this marks the first non-domestic flight he has tried on the airline.

OK. Fine. But "blessed"?

Certainly. In fact, he will tell you exactly *that* every time.

"I'm extremely lucky, even blessed, to be doing what I do," said Bauzá, who, since 2002, has been employed for a decade-plus by Minor League Baseball (MiLB).

Bauzá described his main job as "one of many hats I wear." The 46-year-old native of Puerto Rico calls Miami home during the four months a year when he is not constantly on the road, not required to report personally on a regular basis to MiLB headquarters across the state in St. Petersburg. Attributable to his assorted titles and responsibilities, five Latin American and Caribbean countries comprise the majority of his destinations: Venezuela, the Dominican Republic, Puerto Rico, Cuba and Mexico.

It is thus interesting that one of the several airlines he flies in and out of Venezuela, his most frequent destination, is Aserca (*Aereo Servicios Carabobo,* or Carabobo Air Services, denoting the Venezuelan state where it is headquartered, which also was the boyhood home of *Blue Hombre* Manny Gonzalez). The airline is a perfect match for The Man of Many Hats because its motto, *"por todo lo alto,"* translates roughly into English as "all over the sky."

As for all those hats on his rack, his current official, dual primary title is Field Evaluator/Instructor, MiLB Umpire Development, and Lead Rules Instructor, MiLB Umpire Training Academy. However, those duties are barely one-half of his daily existence; other responsibilities include: Director of the Caribbean World Series for *Confederacion de Beisbol Profesional del Caribe (CPBC)*; Director of Umpiring for the CPBC; and member of the Umpiring Baseball Commission of the World Baseball Softball Confederation (WBSC).

Bauzá, who helps supervise the MiLB academy each offseason, during most of January, at the former Dodgertown spring training complex in Vero Beach, Fla., worked as a minor league umpire for nine years, from 1993-2002. The leagues where he officiated were, in reverse, chronological order, beginning with the most recent listed first: AAA International, AA Eastern, A-Advanced Florida State, "Straight-A" South Atlantic and Rookie Gulf Coast. Additionally, he was invited to do both the Puerto Rican and Caribbean versions of the World Series.

While some – e.g., retired American League umpire Rich Garcia, a close Bauzá friend but also the descendant of Cuban immigrants to Florida – saw the 1999 Major League Baseball-sanctioned exhibition trip to Cuba by the Baltimore Orioles as what Garcia termed a "disgrace," the long-time MiLB staffer looks back on *his* initial sojourn to the Communist-ruled island nation in summer 2015 as "a great opportunity to teach. They have the talents; they need guidance," Bauzá said. That occurred on the heels of the Obama administration's unilateral executive action announcing it intended to warm relations with the Castro regime, which has been in power since 1960, and subject to a U.S. trade and travel embargo during most of that tenure. A follow-up major league exhibition to the '99 trip was a companion to the recent Obama overtures, with the Tampa Bay Rays defeating the Cuban National Team in Havana in spring 2016 – doubtlessly causing Rich Garcia to do another slow burn, even though two of his protégés, Angel Hernández and Laz Díaz, were the event's MLB umpire representatives.

Because Bauzá's purview while wearing one specific hat requires uniformity among Caribbean-Rim countries regarding application of baseball rules, among which are particular umpire guidelines, he believes Cuba needs to be the fifth puzzle piece to be firmly in place, politics aside.

Due to its status as the Caribbean's largest (almost 41,000 square miles) and most populous (11 million-plus) island country – and its strategic location just 90 miles from the nearest U.S. shore – baseball-savvy minds concur there are two inherently intertwined factors underscoring Cuba's importance to the sport. First, baseball has been deeply ingrained in the Cuban experience for so long, regardless of government type. Second, it is generally accepted that, if Cuba were free, it conceivably could someday supplant Venezuela as the largest provider of both player and umpire talent from Latin America for the major leagues and the rest of U.S. professional baseball.

Across the big sea to the west and south, respectively, lie Mexico and Venezuela, both much larger in area and population than Cuba, but non-island nations, each with sun-drenched *Caribe* coastlines. Both boast much more versatile economies than Cuba. As a result, despite *beisbol loco* fervor in all three lands, the two larger entities offer enough diversions to allow natives and visitors to take the sport perhaps relatively more for granted than the Cubans do. Just do not express out loud the sentiment to *Venezolanos* that they take such a heartfelt part of the national fiber *"por sentado"* or "for granted."

In Venezuela in late 2015, a sea change began taking place. In this case, though, the tidal movement had turned in an entirely different direction. Disgruntled Venezuelan voters threw out the long-ruling socialist majority in the national legislature, leaving the new, more conservative politicos to confound sitting President Nicolas Maduro. Maduro is a protégé of late dictator Hugo Chavez, both dyed-in-the-wool left-wingers, and close friends and political soulmates of Fidel Castro and brother Raul, who have ruled Cuba with an iron hand for a half-century-plus.

Rich Garcia, not an overtly political person, yet seemingly the philosophical opposite of Maduro and the Castros, based on the ex-MLB umpire/umpire supervisor's varied unfiltered, even courageous, pronouncements, has a theory on the baseball picture in that South American land sitting on the sunny southern shore of the Caribbean.

"The safest place to be in Venezuela is a baseball game," he said. Despite ongoing political battles, Garcia admitted he "never felt any danger at ballparks." Having ventured to different parts of that nation to conduct instructional clinics and size up the talent base for new umpires on a few trips to the seaside locale, he has seen many places with armed guards or a heavy military presence. However, Garcia said Venezuelan government leaders have ensured that such a show of arms will not occur inside stadium turnstiles. "Chavez was terrible … (but) he didn't mess with baseball," said the descendant of Cuban immigrants to Florida, adding that he was "glad" when the so-called *Chavista* legislative majority was sacked.

Regardless of which party runs the show, though, Venezuela's education system is comparatively more advanced than those in, say, the Dominican Republic and Mexico. Moreover, Garcia said he encounters more proficient English speakers in Venezuela than he has in other countries where the primary language is Spanish.

He gives much of the credit for finding and nurturing each new crop of *Blue Hombres* to the ever-present Bauzá.

"He does a very good job with the Latin kids. They respect him," Garcia said.

***

Of the umpteen decisions and dilemmas Jorge Bauzá faces on a daily basis – regardless of which tropical target he is aiming at the moment – the most-vexing is: *"At what speed do I proceed today?"* There is no language barrier whatsoever to create costly "lost in translation" moments, because Puerto Rico-born Bauzá's native tongue is Spanish. No, it is the complexity, coupled with instability and unpredictability, associated with the governments with which he must deal in most earmarked countries.

Almost literally, from one day to the next, it is difficult to predict which way political winds will blow. Were it not for vast oil resources and revenue – even in times like the relative downturn that continued to grip the energy sector in 2016 – one wonders how relatively stable the big "bananas" of targeted republics would be, especially Venezuela and Mexico.

It is amid this uncertain socio-political atmosphere, then, that the "Umpire Hunter" must try to stay constantly on the move, at as fast a gait as his trusted tennis shoes will take him. The calming effect provided by an easy-paced sport like *beisbol*, the ALL-American pastime (North, South and Central), is an antidote to external strife and turmoil, as underscored by Rich Garcia's "safest place" contention. Of course, no one should ever forget that the inherent, internal peace, once inside a stadium's sanctity, is maintained mainly by *Blue Hombres* – who do not need rifles, pistols, or even badges. Just give each of them a blue-and-gray clothing ensemble, protective black shoes, all the necessary gear to cover them from head to toe and … don't forget the clicker and ball bag. The only commands they need to bark out are: "Play ball, time, ball, strike, safe, out."

With that, it is incumbent upon Jorge Bauzá – and other baseball minds in skyscraper suites in Manhattan and St. Petersburg – to continue keeping one eye on Venezuela, while casting the other eye toward that sleeping giant, Mexico. Peace and stability lie in the balance. Just leave the umpires alone to do it, but first, go find them.

11
MÉXICO OLÉ!
UNLIMITED HORIZONS FOR FUTURE

Mexico is a populous country with great baseball tradition, target-rich with talent in the sport, and anxious to see its countrymen increase their numbers in Major League Baseball (MLB).

From one standpoint, though, that is more dream-like than realistic; Jorge Bauzá would prefer expansion in recruitment of future MLB umpires – *Blue Hombres* – to stretch to every Western Hemisphere country, or basically any place some young kids are able to have bats, balls and gloves, and find some vacant lot on which to play.

Bauzá, despite the visionary projections in his heart, nonetheless is a realist who knows precisely in his keen, analytical mind where the immediate action exists – the Republic of Mexico. At the beginning of the 2016 regular season, the country that shares a 2,000-mile border with its larger neighbor to the north had contributed more than 100 players to the major leagues since Mexico native Mel Almada was the pacesetter in 1933. A trickle of talent followed the outfielder, who graduated from high school in Los Angeles, for a couple of decades, with World War II and the Korean Conflict intervening, until a flood of Mexican talent greatly increasing the flow began in the 1950s, and the subsequent wave has not subsided since.

Hence, it makes sense to mine the *plato y oro* (gold and silver) mother lode available in the country of an estimated 128 million people, and sluice through the metal pan to produce new umpires, notably those of Latino descent who demonstrate at least reasonable English-speaking proficiency coupled with willingness to learn and improve.

"Right now, the main focus has been on Venezuela, Puerto Rico and the Dominican Republic," said Bauzá, a native of Puerto Rico who runs the overall Minor League Baseball (MiLB) Umpire Development Program, with special emphasis on all the growing countries in Latin America and the Caribbean.

"We're trying to expand – to Mexico, mainly – to bring in umpires in the next couple of years. With the recent warming of relationships with Cuba, there also is a lot of potential there as well."

Moreover, in the stepped-up push for Latinos, given the ever-growing Spanish-speaking market, both domestically and externally, the former nine-year MiLB arbiter likewise envisions international recruitment from English-speaking locales where the sport's popularity is up, citing Australia as a prime example. As well as U.S. professional leagues have done in attracting quality umpiring talent in Venezuela, Cuba, the Dominican Republic and Puerto Rico, their combined population of about 60 million is less than one-half of Mexico's – leaving Bauzá and his MLB and MiLB colleagues salivating every time they hear "Mexico" mentioned.

The two-game exhibition series in Mexico City two weeks before the 2016 regular season started was an additional sign of eagerness to pluck umpire prospects from that country. The pair of weekend games in March 2016 matching the Houston Astros against the San Diego Padres – a short series in which each won a game – drew record crowds to the Mexican capital's *Estadio Fray Nano*.

In addition to home-grown umpires, who are prime prospects to become MLB *Blue Hombres* someday, currently working in the unaffiliated AAA-level Mexican League, the two-game set was led calling balls and strikes by Alfonso Marquez, first Mexican-born major league umpire. Plus, helping spearhead the organization of the latest match-up of MLB squads in *La Republica* was Astros' General Manager Jeff Luhnow, who was born and raised in Mexico City.

The new crop of young, eager *árbitros* now calling games in the Mexican League is encouraging as well because of an incredible work ethic, coupled with the fact that competent umpires, regardless of national origin, love the game; they deem as a bonus they are being paid to officiate.

"Mexico has a group of umpires who work the *entire* year – summer league and winter league," Bauzá proclaimed, with an extra shot of enthusiasm. The idea, he added, is to "get 'em young and bring 'em to the States."

It is win-win, in his estimation, because "the dream of being a major league umpire is an important thing – to reach that goal," said Bauzá, who spent the week prior to the Astros-Padres games on his most recent scouting mission into the country's three largest population centers of Guadalajara, Monterrey and the capital itself.

As for achieving goals, Bauzá and his higher-ups and peers in the MLB and MiLB offices – all the way to the 31st-floor suite at 245 Park Ave., in midtown Manhattan, where Commissioner of Baseball Rob Manfred sits – share a specific goal: "We hope to have five solid Mexican umpires in the system, regardless of level, within five years" via the Umpire Development System (UDS) Bauzá helped devise. "It takes several years to develop (a single) prospect after identifying each individual," he emphasized.

Wherever professional baseball is played, a country's size notwithstanding, "you'll find a good pool of talent," Bauzá said. "Regardless, we still need more exposure in Mexico. It's real encouraging so far, (but) we need to add another step to the process," added the chief umpire talent hunter, who nonetheless is essentially a one-man show, albeit not a one-trick *caballito*, being that he has more ideas and options available to "pony up."

For instance, as of spring 2016, the next logical moment to have added some extra *salsa* to the mix could have been from September 2016 through March 2017, as the World Baseball Congress (WBC) tournament was to be played all over the globe – even in the most unimaginable places.

"Panama, maybe?" Bauzá speculated – *con razon* (with reason). "Panama has started a conversation. Also, we've had a couple of Aussies in the system. We have a good relationship with the Australian League."

In addition, Bauzá – who never sleeps much, anyway – keeps his eyes and ears open north of the border, hoping to find more eager, young, competent *Blue Mounties* like the Pride of Saskatchewan, current MLB call-up umpire Stu Scheurwater.

Naturally, still going strong is Venezuela, which has been by far the chief font of non-domestic talent over the past decade or less, with at least a half-dozen supremely qualified *Venezolano* umpires either working at the MLB or MiLB levels. As Rich Garcia, baseball's longest-tenured *Blue Hombre*, never stops reminding everyone, Venezuelan ballparks are indeed "safe zones" amid other turmoil. Therefore, ever-shifting political winds there are unlikely to retard the current momentum – a theory which applies positively to the Dominican Republic, only on a smaller scale. Nor should anyone ever take lightly Bauzá's birthplace, Puerto Rico.

Then the big Caribbean "elephant in the room," Cuba, must be watched carefully as a Wild Card in the umpire sweepstakes, contingent on how recent political "noise" will affect the vision of someone like Jorge Bauzá.

The still-with-skeptics idea of instant review, or instant *replay*, which was unveiled and used in 2015, remains a factor of potential stress and strife – especially if there is a more accelerated addition of on-field officials whose first language is not English.

One only needs to refer back to Chapter 1 of *this* book and the plight of Cuban *émigré* Armando Rodriguez, MLB's original *Blue Hombre*. His relatively rapid demise was attributable to several reasons. However, the two key negatives were his unwillingness to master American English and his adamant refusal consequently to learn how to complete critical incident reports.

With that in mind, Jorge Bauzá, who grew up with Spanish as his native tongue and had to overcome many hurdles to achieve his current status by working hard, being persistent and abiding by common-sense rules, is only trying to be fair with everyone involved – no matter what are their individual stations in life.

As a result, he believes there is absolutely no reason or excuse for anyone desirous of someday wanting to achieve the pinnacle of baseball umpiring not to adhere to the following basic requirements (which are an updated enhancement of those listed in the Introduction):

- Have a basic knowledge of English, with potential for improvement;
- Demonstrate the ability to communicate clearly and quickly;

- Understand strict time limitations, especially regarding Instant Review;
- Demonstrate the ability to act instinctively, as needed, in making split-second decisions or responses;
- Maintain excellent physical condition;
- High school diploma or GED;
- Reasonable body weight;
- 20/20 vision (with or without glasses or contact lenses);
- Strong interpersonal skills;
- Good communication skills;
- Quick reflexes and good coordination;
- Some athletic ability;
- Facial hair: None preferred unless well-trimmed;
- Required preliminary training for the job (i.e., professional umpire school).

***

Even as noteworthy and applicable all these rules and guidelines are, though, it all goes back to one of the five Spanish words that propelled us into telling "The Legend of the *Blue Hombres*" to begin with: *pasión*.

As Gerry Davis, a living umpire legend himself, very succinctly put it: "There's so much passion for baseball in Latin countries."

Along with that passion, current and future *Blue Hombres* all over the hemisphere also were learning they could accomplish even more in a high-tech manner. However, that is an ongoing story that will continue to unfold.

SOURCE NOTES

Introduction

The Baseball Cube, Cohen, Gary, *Montreal, Quebec, Canada,* 2015

Society for American Baseball Research, Crimmins School for Journalism and Mass Communications, Arizona State University, *Tempe and Phoenix, Ariz.,* 2015

Baseball Research Journal, Crimmins School for Journalism and Mass Communications, Arizona State University, Tempe and Phoenix, Ariz., 2015

"The Secrets of Major League Baseball," Ethics Corner column, Wolper, Allan, *Editor & Publisher*, April 18, 2002

Baseball-Reference.com, various citations and references, including box scores, standings and results et al, 1901-Present

BaseballAlmanac.com, website, 2015-16

Umpire Roster , *MLB.com*, Official Site of Major League Baseball, 2016

"Rich Garcia Joins PBUC Staff," MLB.com, ibid., May 19, 2010

"These Umpires and Referees Are Best Known for Botched Calls. Here's How They Made Peace with Their Legacies," Schultz, Jordan, *HuffingtonPost*.com, March 6, 2015

"Big League Baseball Returns to Cuba," Walker, Ben, *Associated Press*, March 27, 1999

"Better Know an Umpire: Angel Campos," Malinowski, Erik, *Deadspin,* May 10, 2012

Major League Umpires' Performance 2007-2010: A Comprehensive Statistical Review, Goldblatt, Andrew, *McFarland,* 2011

Umpire-Empire.com, website, July 17, 2015

"Umpire Rosters for Minor League Baseball," *Referee magazine,* January 2016

The Pride of Havana: A History of Cuban Baseball, Echevarria, Roberto Gonzáles, *Oxford University Press*, 2001

"No Lie: This Polygraph Specialist Weeds Out the Dishonest," Hardesty, Greg, *Behind the Badge OC, Anaheim P.D., Cornerstone Communications*, Aug. 7, 2014

"UEFL Umpire Profiles Updated for 2016 Season," *Close Call Sports*, Jan. 28, 2016

Retrosheet.org, baseball statistical history and research, independent website, 2015-16

"De Jesus Debuts as First MLB Umpire from Dominican Republic," Bower, David, *MLB.com,* April 22, 2016

"MLB's First Dominican Umpire De Jesus in Indians-Tigers Series," Townsend, Mark, *Big League Stew, Yahoo Sports,* April 22, 2016

"Major League Baseball Has First Dominican Umpire," *Dominican Today,* April 19, 2016, and *Associated Press,* April, 23, 2016

Encyclopedia of Minor League Baseball, 2nd Edition, Johnson, Lloyd, and Wolff, Miles, Editors, *Baseball America,* 1997

The 2016 MLB Umpire Media Guide, Teevan, Michael, and Muller, Donald, Editors, *MLB Communications,* 2016

Chapter 1

Encyclopedia of Minor League Baseball, 2nd Edition, Johnson, Lloyd, and Wolff, Miles, Editors, *Baseball America,* 1997, ibid.

Retrosheet.org, baseball statistical history and research, independent website, 2015-16, ibid.

The 2016 MLB Umpire Media Guide, Teevan, Michael, and Muller, Donald, Editors, *MLB Communications,* 2016, ibid.

The Baseball Cube, Cohen, Gary, *Montreal, Quebec, Canada,* 2015, ibid.

Baseball-Reference.com, various citations and references, including box scores, standings and results et al, 1901-Present, ibid.

BaseballAlmanac.com, website, 2015-16, ibid.

Umpire Roster,MLB.com, Official Site of Major League Baseball, 2016, ibid.

The Pride of Havana: A History of Cuban Baseball, Echevarria, Roberto Gonzáles, *Oxford University Press,* 2001, ibid.

"Obituary: Danny McDevitt," New York Times, **Nov. 24, 2010**

"Big League Baseball Returns to Cuba," Walker, Ben, *Associated Press*, **March 27, 1999, ibid.**

"UEFL Umpire Profiles Updated for 2016 Season," Close Call Sports, **Jan. 28, 2016, ibid.**

Umpire-Empire.com, website, **July 17, 2015, ibid.**

"Umpire Rosters for Minor League Baseball," Referee magazine, **January 2016, ibid.**

"Rich Garcia Joins PBUC Staff," MLB.com, ibid., **May 19, 2010, ibid.**

Chapter 2

"Say It Ain't So, Vincent," O'Keeffe, Michael, **July 29, 2007**

The Baseball Cube, Cohen, Gary, *Montreal, Quebec, Canada*, **2015, ibid.**

"Report: Gambling Touched Baseball Umpires," Pete Brush, *Associated Press*, **March 8, 2002**

The 2016 MLB Umpire Media Guide, Teevan, Michael, and Muller, Donald, Editors, *MLB Communications*, **2016, ibid.**

Encyclopedia of Minor League Baseball, 2nd Edition, Johnson, Lloyd, and Wolff, Miles, Editors, *Baseball America*, **1997, ibid.**

Retrosheet.org, baseball statistical history and research, independent website, **2015-16, ibid.**

The 2016 MLB Umpire Media Guide, Teevan, Michael, and Muller, Donald, Editors, *MLB Communications,* 2016, ibid.

The Baseball Cube, Cohen, Gary, *Montreal, Quebec, Canada,* 2015, ibid.

Baseball-Reference.com, various citations and references, including box scores, standings and results et al, 1901-Present, ibid.

BaseballAlmanac.com, website, 2015-16, ibid.

Umpire Roster, *LB.com*, Official Site of Major League Baseball, 2016, ibid.

"Michael Pineda Ejected from Yankees-Red Sox Game After Foreign Substance Discovered," Associated Press, April 23, 2014

The Pride of Havana: A History of Cuban Baseball, Echevarria, Roberto Gonzáles, *Oxford University Press*, 2001, ibid.

"Big League Baseball Returns to Cuba," Walker, Ben, *Associated Press*, March 27, 1999, ibid.

"UEFL Umpire Profiles Updated for 2016 Season," Close Call Sports, Jan. 28, 2016, ibid.

Umpire-Empire.com, website, July 17, 2015, ibid.

"Umpire Rosters for Minor League Baseball," Referee magazine, January 2016, ibid.

"Rich Garcia Joins PBUC Staff," MLB.com, ibid., May 19, 2010, ibid.

"Nolan Ryan – Robin Ventura: Inside Story of Baseball's Most Famous Fight," Goldman, Rob, *The Post Game,* excerpted from *Nolan Ryan: Making*

of a Pitcher, Goldman, Rob, *Triumph Books,* 2014

"Umpire's Bad Call Recalls Maier Incident in '96," Curry, Jack, *New York Times,* Oct. 11, 2009

"Winning with a Boy's Help, Yankees Make No Apologies," Curry, Jack, *New York Times,* Oct. 10, 1996

"A Night for Redemption," (commentary), Lupica, Mike, *New York Daily News,* Oct. 18, 1998

"League American," *Baseball Library,* 2015

Wayback Machine, Internet Archive, Feb. 2, 2007, retrieved December 2015

"It's a Long Road from Umpiring School to the Majors," Pentz, Perry D., *Herald-Tribune,* July 23, 2006

"MLB Exec Solomon Resigns," Fordin, Spencer, *MLB News,* June 7, 2012

"MLB Fires Jimmie Lee Solomon," Leventhal, Josh, *Baseball America,* June 5, 2012

"MLB Fires Longtime Exec Jimmie Lee Solomon," Nightengale, Ben, *USA Today,* June 6, 2012

"Jimmie Lee Solomon's Departure from Major Leagues," *International Business Times,* June 10, 2012

Official Baseball Rules, 2015 Edition, Recodified, Reorganized, and Amended for 2015

Colorado General Assembly, *Legislative Information,* 2016 Regular Session

Chapter 3

"Instant Replay Goes Off without a Hitch," Bloom, Barry M., *MLB.com,* Sept. 4, 2008

Encyclopedia of Minor League Baseball, 2nd Edition, Johnson, Lloyd, and Wolff, Miles, Editors, *Baseball America*, 1997, **ibid.**

Retrosheet.org, baseball statistical history and research, independent website, 2015-16, ibid.

The 2016 MLB Umpire Media Guide, Teevan, Michael, and Muller, Donald, Editors, *MLB Communications,* 2016, **ibid.**

The Baseball Cube, Cohen, Gary, *Montreal, Quebec, Canada,* 2015, **ibid.**

Baseball-Reference.com, various citations and references, including box scores, standings and results et al, **1901-Present, ibid.**

BaseballAlmanac.com, website, 2015-16, **ibid.**

Umpire Roster , *MLB.com*, Official Site of Major League Baseball, **2016, ibid.**

"UEFL Umpire Profiles Updated for 2016 Season," *Close Call Sports*, **Jan.** 28, 2016, ibid.

Umpire-Empire.com, website, July 17, 2015, ibid.

"Umpire Rosters for Minor League Baseball," *Referee magazine,* January 2016, ibid.

Chapter 4

Encyclopedia of Minor League Baseball, 2nd Edition, Johnson, Lloyd, and Wolff, Miles, Editors, *Baseball America*, 1997, ibid.

Retrosheet.org, baseball statistical history and research, independent website, 2015-16, ibid.

The 2016 MLB Umpire Media Guide, Teevan, Michael, and Muller, Donald, Editors, *MLB Communications*, 2016, ibid.

The Baseball Cube, Cohen, Gary, *Montreal, Quebec, Canada*, 2015, ibid.

Baseball-Reference.com, various citations and references, including box scores, standings and results et al, 1901-Present, ibid.

BaseballAlmanac.com, website, 2015-16, ibid.

Umpire Roster , *MLB.com*, Official Site of Major League Baseball, 2016, ibid.

"*UEFL Umpire Profiles Updated for 2016 Season,*" *Close Call Sports*, Jan. 28, 2016, ibid.

Umpire-Empire.com, website, July 17, 2015, ibid.

CoastalPlain.com, Official Website of the Coastal Plain League, Hilliard, Shelby, April 21, 2016

"*Umpire Rosters for Minor League Baseball,*" *Referee magazine*, January 2016, ibid.

"*Better Know an Umpire: Laz Diaz,* "Malinowski, Erik, *Deadspin*, April 30, 2012

"Umpire Laz Diaz Does Salsa Dance with Phillie Phanatic," Yahoo Sports Staff, *Yahoo.com,* **Aug. 7, 2014**

"Fan Attacks Umpire at Royals-White Sox Game," Gano, Rick, *Associated Press,* **April, 16, 2003**

"Laz Diaz Profile," *DigPlanet.com,* **March 2016**

"Russell Martin Says Umpire Laz Diaz Wouldn't Let Him Throw Ball Back to Pitcher After Yankees Question Calls on Balls and Strikes," Feinsand, Mark, *New York Daily News,* **May 31, 2012**

"Forbes: The World's Billionaires, Arturo Moreno," *Forbes magazine,* **March 2013**

"Storied Stadiums," Smith, Curt, *Nye: Carroll,* **2001**

Chapter 5

"Umpire State of Mind," Bliss, Jeff, *Cal State EastBay,* seasonal collegiate alumni magazine, **Spring 2016**

Encyclopedia of Minor League Baseball, 2ⁿᵈ Edition, Johnson, Lloyd, and Wolff, Miles, Editors, *Baseball America,* **1997, ibid.**

Retrosheet.org, baseball statistical history and research, independent website, **2015-16, ibid.**

The 2016 MLB Umpire Media Guide, Teevan, Michael, and Muller, Donald, Editors, *MLB Communications,* **2016, ibid.**

The Baseball Cube, Cohen, Gary, *Montreal, Quebec, Canada,* **2015, ibid.**

"Umpire Blazes Trail," Ponsi, Lou, *Orange County Register,* July 8, 2007

"Lest Ye Be Judged," Mooallea, Jon, *ESPN The Magazine,* June 20, 2014

Baseball-Reference.com, various citations and references, including box scores, standings and results et al, **1901-Present, ibid.**

BaseballAlmanac.com, website, **2015-16, ibid.**

Umpire Roster , *MLB.com,* Official Site of Major League Baseball, **2016, ibid.**

"UEFL Umpire Profiles Updated for 2016 Season," *Close Call Sports,* Jan. 28, 2016, ibid.

Umpire-Empire.com, website, July 17, 2015, ibid.

"Umpire Rosters for Minor League Baseball," *Referee magazine,* January 2016, ibid.

Chapter 6

Encyclopedia of Minor League Baseball, 2nd Edition, Johnson, Lloyd, and Wolff, Miles, Editors, *Baseball America,* **1997, ibid.**

Retrosheet.org, baseball statistical history and research, independent website, **2015-16, ibid.**

The 2016 MLB Umpire Media Guide, Teevan, Michael, and Muller, Donald, Editors, *MLB Communications,* **2016, ibid.**

The Baseball Cube, Cohen, Gary, *Montreal, Quebec, Canada,* **2015, ibid.**

Baseball-Reference.com, various citations and references, including box scores, standings and results et al, **1901-Present, ibid.**

BaseballAlmanac.com, website, **2015-16, ibid.**

Umpire Roster , *MLB.com*, Official Site of Major League Baseball, **2016, ibid.**

"UEFL Umpire Profiles Updated for 2016 Season," Close Call Sports, **Jan. 28, 2016, ibid.**

Umpire-Empire.com, website, **July 17, 2015, ibid.**

"Umpire Rosters for Minor League Baseball," Referee magazine, **January 2016, ibid.**

"Roster: 2014 MLB Japan All-Star Series," Close Call Sports and UEFL, **Nov. 11, 2014**

Chapter 7

"Home Plate Umpire Takes Flying Bat to Face Mask," Erisa, Mike, Baseball Writer, *CBSSports.com,* **July 9, 2014**

"Plate Umpire Danley Leaves Game After Foul Off His Facemask," Associated Press, **May 13, 2016**

Encyclopedia of Minor League Baseball, 2nd Edition, Johnson, Lloyd, and Wolff, Miles, Editors, *Baseball America,* **1997, ibid.**

Retrosheet.org, baseball statistical history and research, independent website, **2015-16, ibid.**

The 2016 MLB Umpire Media Guide, Teevan, Michael, and Muller, Donald, Editors, *MLB Communications,* 2016, ibid.

The Baseball Cube, Cohen, Gary, *Montreal, Quebec, Canada,* 2015, ibid.

Baseball-Reference.com, various citations and references, including box scores, standings and results et al, 1901-Present, ibid.

BaseballAlmanac.com, website, 2015-16, ibid.

Umpire Roster , *MLB.com*, Official Site of Major League Baseball, 2016, ibid.

"UEFL Umpire Profiles Updated for 2016 Season," Close Call Sports, Jan. 28, 2016, ibid.

Umpire-Empire.com, website, July 17, 2015, ibid.

"Umpire Rosters for Minor League Baseball," Referee magazine, January 2016, ibid.

Chapter 8

Encyclopedia of Minor League Baseball, 2nd *Edition*, Johnson, Lloyd, and Wolff, Miles, Editors, *Baseball America*, 1997, ibid.

Retrosheet.org, baseball statistical history and research, independent website, 2015-16, ibid.

The 2016 MLB Umpire Media Guide, Teevan, Michael, and Muller, Donald, Editors, *MLB Communications,* 2016, ibid.

The Baseball Cube, Cohen, Gary, *Montreal, Quebec, Canada,* 2015, ibid.

Baseball-Reference.com, various citations and references, including box scores, standings and results et al, 1901-Present, ibid.

BaseballAlmanac.com, website, 2015-16, ibid.

Umpire Roster , *MLB.com*, Official Site of Major League Baseball, 2016, ibid.

"De Jesus Debuts As First MLB Umpire from Dominican Republic," Bower, David, *MLB.com,* April 22, 2016, ibid.

"MLB's First Dominican Umpire De Jesus in Indians-Tigers Series," Townsend, Mark, *Big League Stew, Yahoo Sports,* April 22, 2016, ibid.

"Major League Baseball Has First Dominican Umpire," *Dominican Today,* April 19, 2016, and *Associated Press,* April, 23, 2016, ibid.

"Better Know an Umpire: Angel Campos," Malinowski, Erik, *Deadspin,* May 10, 2012, ibid.

"UEFL Umpire Profiles Updated for 2016 Season," *Close Call Sports,* Jan. 28, 2016, ibid.

Umpire-Empire.com, website, July 17, 2015, ibid.

"Umpire Rosters for Minor League Baseball," *Referee magazine,* January 2016, ibid.

Chapter 9

Encyclopedia of Minor League Baseball, 2nd Edition, Johnson, Lloyd, and Wolff, Miles, Editors, *Baseball America*, 1997, ibid.

Retrosheet.org, baseball statistical history and research, independent website, 2015-16, ibid.

The 2016 MLB Umpire Media Guide, Teevan, Michael, and Muller, Donald, Editors, *MLB Communications*, 2016, ibid.

The Baseball Cube, Cohen, Gary, *Montreal, Quebec, Canada*, 2015, ibid.

"No Lie: This Polygraph Specialist Weeds Out the Dishonest," Hardesty, Greg, *Behind the Badge OC, Anaheim P.D., Cornerstone Communications*, Aug. 7, 2014

Baseball-Reference.com, various citations and references, including box scores, standings and results et al, 1901-Present, ibid.

BaseballAlmanac.com, website, 2015-16, ibid.

Umpire Roster , *MLB.com*, Official Site of Major League Baseball, 2016, ibid.

"UEFL Umpire Profiles Updated for 2016 Season," *Close Call Sports*, Jan. 28, 2016, ibid.

"Four Winds, Silver Hawks Strike 10-Year Deal," Lotra, Al, *South Bend Tribune*, Sept. 21, 2013

"Angels' Physician Retiring," *Los Angeles Times*, Jan. 19, 1995

Umpire-Empire.com, website, July 17, 2015, ibid.

"Umpire Rosters for Minor League Baseball," Referee magazine, January 2016, ibid.

Chapter 10

"2016 Houston Astros Media Information," Mexico City Series, Spring Training, 2016

"MLB Opening Office in Mexico City," USA Today, March 24, 2016

Retrosheet.org, baseball statistical history and research, independent website, 2015-16, ibid.

"Exhibition Enhancing MLB Ties to Mexico," op-ed column, Justice, Richard, *MLB.com,* March 26, 2016

The Baseball Cube, Cohen, Gary, *Montreal, Quebec, Canada,* 2015, ibid.

"UEFL Umpire Profiles Updated for 2016 Season," Close Call Sports, Jan. 28, 2016, ibid.

The Pride of Havana: A History of Cuban Baseball, Echevarria, Roberto Gonzáles, *Oxford University Press,* 2001, ibid.

"Big League Baseball Returns to Cuba," Walker, Ben, *Associated Press,* March 27, 1999, ibid.

Encyclopedia of Minor League Baseball, 2nd Edition, Johnson, Lloyd, and Wolff, Miles, Editors, *Baseball America,* 1997, ibid.

The 2016 MLB Umpire Media Guide, Teevan, Michael, and Muller, Donald, Editors, *MLB Communications,* 2016, ibid.

Baseball-Reference.com, various citations and references, including box scores, standings and results et al, 1901-Present, ibid.

BaseballAlmanac.com, website, 2015-16, ibid.

Umpire Roster, *MLB.com*, Official Site of Major League Baseball, 2016, ibid.

"UEFL Umpire Profiles Updated for 2016 Season," *Close Call Sports*, Jan. 28, 2016, ibid.

Umpire-Empire.com, website, July 17, 2015, ibid.

"Umpire Rosters for Minor League Baseball," *Referee magazine*, January 2016, ibid.

Chapter 11

Encyclopedia of Minor League Baseball, 2nd Edition, Johnson, Lloyd, and Wolff, Miles, Editors, *Baseball America*, 1997, ibid.

Retrosheet.org, baseball statistical history and research, independent website, 2015-16, ibid.

The 2016 MLB Umpire Media Guide, Teevan, Michael, and Muller, Donald, Editors, *MLB Communications,* 2016, ibid.

The Baseball Cube, Cohen, Gary, *Montreal, Quebec, Canada,* 2015, ibid.

Baseball-Reference.com, various citations and references, including box scores, standings and results et al, 1901-Present, ibid.

BaseballAlmanac.com, website, 2015-16, ibid.

Umpire Roster , *MLB.com*, Official Site of Major League Baseball, **2016**, **ibid.**

"UEFL Umpire Profiles Updated for 2016 Season," *Close Call Sports*, **Jan. 28, 2016, ibid.**

"Big League Baseball Returns to Cuba," Walker, Ben, *Associated Press*, **March 27, 1999, ibid.**

Umpire-Empire.com, website, **July 17, 2015, ibid.**

"Umpire Rosters for Minor League Baseball," *Referee magazine,* **January 2016, ibid.**

Index

WBSC Umpiring Baseball Commission, 154

WebMD.com, 130

Wegner, Mark, 76, 114, 124

Welke, Bill, 62, 92, 126, 131

Welke, Tim, 62, 131

Wendelstedt, Harry, 21, 77, 81, 131

Wendelstedt, Hunter, 21, 81, 146, 131

Wendelstedt Umpire School, 21, 81, 149

West Coast circuit, 150

West, "Country" Joe, 4, 70, 116, 122, 124, 127

W. Roosevelt Boulevard (Key West), 38

Western Athletic Conference (WAC), 133

Western Hemisphere, 159

Western Kentucky (region), 97

"whoop-ass," 79

"wide-open," 150

Williams, Art, 94

Wilson, Willie, 41

Winters, Mike, 75, 114, 119, 124

Wisconsin, 139

Wolf, Jim, 125, 127-128

Wolf, Randy, 125

Wolters, Tony, 125

World Baseball Congress (WBC) Tournament 2006/2007, 161

World Baseball Softball Confederation (WBSC), 133, 154

World Series, 18, 50, 55-57, 63, 67-68, 77, 83-84, 95-96, 125, 137-138, 171

World Umpire Association (WUA), 4

World War II, 145, 159

Wrigley Field, 127-128

Y

Yankee Stadium, 38, 42, 106

Yeager, Chuck, 8

Yeager, Steve, 8

Yeager throat protector, 8

Yonto, Joe, Sr., 140

Yonto, Joe, Jr., 139-141

Young, Larry, 45-47

Z

Zacatecas state, Mexico, 83-84, 97, 102

Zayos, Mónico, 125

ACKNOWLEDGMENTS

The first name that popped into my head when the inspiration to delve into a topic heretofore given little, if any, exposure was Rich Garcia. As many times as my hunches have been way off-target, I'm glad to tell you this one definitely was a bulls-eye. Despite some initial skepticism, Garcia, now retired but still the longest-serving Latino umpire in big league history, was anxious to work with me and unselfishly share his seemingly endless list of contacts in the baseball world in general, but more specifically in the tight, much narrower realm of umpires, past and present.

Once added confidence with Rich was engendered – especially considering my 18 years as a college and high school umpire in the 1980s and '90s – he got me in touch with Jorge Bauzá, whose role among arbiters is well-documented on the pages herein. Jorge is the closest thing to being a *guru* among all minor league umpires and particularly with prospects all over Latin America; I honestly believe he has a cell number and email address for each individual with *any* direct or indirect connection to the minor leagues.

It was therefore noteworthy that this early, and ongoing, connection with Rich and Jorge made the journey much smoother than originally anticipated. Thus, after they "opened the gate," I was able, over a period of months, to snag interviews with others to whom I will be eternally grateful and who helped make a good book better; among others, they include Gerry Davis, Laz Díaz, Alfonso "Fonzy" Marquez, Bill Haller, Vince Delgado, Ken Franek and, of course, Rich and Jorge themselves.

I also extend much gratitude to those who had a great hand in the book's preparation – editing, beta-reading and just general feedback. Mostly, they are Chuck Swift, Mike Pinchot, Linda East, Jim Benton, Charlotte Henley Babb and, of course, "Goob." A special kudo is tossed the way of the talented Brandon McElhinney, who designed the book's entertaining front and back covers, which entices any reader to open it and travel virtually side-by-side with the *Blue Hombres*. It was then my job to keep curious readers turning page after page. Brandon is a real trouper – a cancer survivor whose mother lost her long battle with Alzheimer's while he was working on finishing the covers.

The new, small imprint of *TRail's End Press©* offers rookie or otherwise unknown authors a vehicle with which to proceed with the dignity normally accorded only famous, best-selling authors whose agents have set them up with major publishing houses. Likewise, I feel fortunate, through referrals and thorough vetting, to have found such competent professionals as Jason and Marina Anderson of Polgarus Studio to do top-notch formatting at a reasonable price.

No one is blessed more than I am to have supportive family members who put up with the varied moods associated with an unpredictable author in their midst. Naturally, the one this applies to most is my beautiful, intelligent, multilingual wife, Maria, who has endured all the bouquets and brickbats alike with me for decades.

PHIL ROSS, ARAPAHOE COUNTY, COLO., JUNE 2016

Made in the USA
Columbia, SC
15 January 2018